ONE DAY
ON THE SOMME

1st July 1916

BARRY CUTTELL

GMS ENTERPRISES

First published 1998
by GMS Enterprises
67 Pyhill, Bretton, Peterborough,
England PE3 8QQ
Tel and Fax (01733) 265123
EMail: GMSAVIATIONBOOKS@ Compuserve.com

ISBN: 1 870384 67 9

A donation from the sale of this book will be made towards
the maintenance of the privately owned memorial of
Lochnagar Crater at La Boisselle on the Somme

Printed and bound for GMS Enterprises

CONTENTS

TO ANN and FRED WARREN
whose contagious interest in those
who fought on the Somme Battlefield
is a joy to share

LIST OF ABBREVIATIONS

Att:	-	attack
Assy.	-	Assembly
Bed./Bedf:	-	Bedfordshire Regiment
B.E.F:	-	British Expeditionary Force
Bet:	-	between
Bords:	-	Borderers
Bn:	-	Battalion
BRIG:	-	Brigade
Buffs:	-	Buffs - East Kent Regiment
C.C.S:	-	Casualty Clearing Station
C.i.C:	-	Commander in Chief
c.m:	-	centimetres
C.O:	-	Commanding Officer
Cont:	-	continuation
Coy:	-	Company
C.W.G.C:	-	Commonwealth War Graves Commission
Dev:	-	Devonshire Regiment
DIV:	-	Division
D.L.I/Dur.L.I:	-	Durham Light Infantry
Dors:	-	Dorset Regiment
D.o.W./Duke of W:	-	Duke of Wellington (West Riding Regiment)
E:	-	East
Fm:	-	Farm
Fors:	-	Foresters (c.f. Sher. Fors.)
Fus:	-	Fusiliers
Gen:	-	General
G.O.C:	-	General Officer Commanding
Gordon H:	-	Gordon Highlanders
Gr. Howards:	-	Green Howards (Yorkshire Regiment)
Hants:	-	Hampshire Regiment
H.L.I:	-	Highland Light Infantry
H.Q:	-	Headquarters
I.G.N:	-	Institut Géographique National
Innis:	-	Royal Inniskilling Fusiliers
I.N.V:	-	Irish National Volunteers
King's:	-	King's Liverpool Regiment
k.m:	-	kilometer(s)
K.O.Y.L.I:	-	King's Own Yorkshire Light Infantry
K.O.S.B:	-	King's Own Scottish Borderers
La:	-	Lane
La Bois:	-	La Boisselle
Lancs. Fus:	-	Lancashire Fusiliers
Lieut:	-	Lieutenant
Lincs:	-	Lincolnshire Regiment
Lon:	-	London Regiment

Lon. Scot:	-	London Scottish - London Regiment
L.R.B:	-	London Rifle Brigade - London Regiment
m:	-	meter(s)
Maj:	-	Major
Man:	-	Manchester Regiment
Middx:	-	Middlesex Regiment
Mon:	-	Monmouthshire Regiment
N:	-	North
N.F./North.Fus:	-	Northumberland Fusiliers
Nor:	-	Norfolk Regiment
North'n:	-	Northampton Regiment
OBJ:	-	Objective
Orig:	-	Original
Pnrs:	-	Pioneers
P.R.O:	-	Public Relations Officer
Q.V.R:	-	Queen Victoria's Rifles - London Regiment
Q.W.R:	-	Queen's Westminster Rifles - London Regiment
R:	-	River
Rif:	-	Rifles
Rif. Brig:	-	Rifle Brigade
Roy:	-	Royal
Roy. Berks:	-	Royal Berkshire Regiment
R.D.F./R.Dub.Fus	-	Royal Dublin Fusiliers
R.Inn.Fus:	-	Royal Inniskilling Fusiliers
R.I.R./R.Ir.R:	-	Royal Irish Rifles
R.Wars/Roy.Wars:	-	Royal Warwickshire Regiment
R.S.F:	-	Royal Scots Fusiliers
R.W.F:	-	Royal Welsh Fusiliers
S:	-	South
Scot. Rif:	-	Scottish Rifles (The Cameronians)
Seaforths/Seaf.H:	-	Seaforth Highlanders
Sher. Fors:	-	Sherwood Foresters (Notts. & Derby Regiment)
S.L.I/Som.L.I:	-	Somerset Light Infantry
Suff:	-	Suffolk Regiment
S.W.B:	-	South Wales Borderers
T./Tr:	-	Trench
Tyn. Ir:	-	Tyneside Irish
Tyn. Scot:	-	Tyneside Scottish
U.V.F:	-	Ulster Volunteer Force
W:	-	West
Wd:	-	Wood
Wilts:	-	Wiltshire Regiment
Worcs:	-	Worcestershire Regiment

LIST OF MAPS

INTRODUCTION

Some of the most frequently asked questions by pilgrims to the Somme, particularly by first-time visitors, are:

"Where was a certain battalion on the day of the Big Push?"

"To which divisions were the various brigades attached?"

"Which division was engaged at a certain sector?"

"What was the official battalion name of one of the "Pals" battalions?"

"Why can't I find the Y Sap crater?"

"Where is the Leipzig Redoubt?/Birch Tree Wood?"

"Where was Campbell Avenue?/Munich Trench?"

Which battalions were in a certain brigade/division?"

Information collected over many years and entered on a card filing system has been computerised, facilitating the production of various indexed lists which provide quick answers to most of these sorts of questions.

Although the divisional order of battle is often quoted in books dealing with this campaign, the author has included full indexed lists of divisions, brigades and battalions, etc. It seemed, therefore, that a guide containing this data would perhaps meet some of the needs of visitors to the battleground. These lists are relative to the first day of the battle, the 1st July, 1916.

The author has also incorporated an alphabetical list of trenches linked to the objectives of the 1st July. The names of some of these trenches were as well-known as the villages which became household names during 1916. I cannot claim the trench list is complete, it grows with each visit. Sites behind the front line used for the training and assembly of troops for later attacks, ammunition and food dumps, C.C.S.'s (casualty clearing stations), fodder for the cavalry, railtrack and sleepers for the construction of new railways, sites for mass burials, all the paraphernalia necessary for the conduct of war cover an area used throughout the whole of the campaign which ended in mid-November, 1916.

It will be noticed that a number of divisions/brigades are marked "in reserve". This is because the data listed is the situation as it was when the whistles were blown and the infantry left the trenches at 7.30am on the 1st July. Many reserve battalions were soon brought into the action and the casualties were often as heavy, and in some cases, heavier, than those in the leading waves. The leading battalions had to face heavy machine gun fire but succeeding waves had to pass through no-man's land not only under machine gun fire but also from the German artillery which had then found the exact range.

Thousands of visitors come each year to the Somme, many of whom are expert and far more experienced than myself and it is not primarily to these experienced researchers, many of whom are my friends, that this book is addressed - although it is very possible that the format of the book would be useful to them while doing their work - but rather to those visitors who come for the first time or are perhaps returning for a second or third visit, possibly to trace the steps of a fallen relative or to find some of the well-known sites on the battlefield and who are unfamiliar with the accessibility of official trench maps and other documentation. This book is intended to be an easy guide to factual information relative to the 1st July and perhaps serve as an introduction to further reading. I have not included details of the many cemeteries which can be visited in the area as there are many guides of this nature. Rose Coombs's *"Before Endeavours Fade"* has been in print for twenty years and the recent guides by Martin and Mary Middlebrook, *"The Somme Battlefields"* and Major & Mrs Holts Battlefield Guide to the Somme are highly recommended.

There is an immense wealth of literature available and today, eighty years on, new books are still being published, many of a very high quality. More often than not, when an initial interest is aroused, it tends to grow and the visitor returns again and again. It is hoped that in some small way this guide will encourage new visitors to take a deeper interest in what has been called "The Blackest Day in British History", to ask "why?", to try to understand. One of the most pleasurable aspects of having such an interest is that visitors all have a common bond, an interest in what happened eighty years ago, and it is always a source of great satisfaction and pleasure to be able to ask about or discuss the latest information on books, trench locations and other relevant topics. There is a feeling of friendship in the Somme, a comradeship reflected so well in the Pals and other battalions which represented the cream of British youth who fought and died for freedom on that tragic first of July on the slopes of Picardy.

A BRIEF SURVEY OF THE ORIGINS OF THE SOMME CAMPAIGN

The name VERDUN is to the French as the SOMME is to the British people and the two have remained inextricably linked. The main German action in 1915 against the French was in Artois and Champagne areas while, on the British front, the battles of Neuve Chapelle, Ypres, Hooge, Festubert and Loos were fought. The German offensive in Serbia and Russia had not brought about the desired results.

At the Chantilly conference at the end of 1915 Marshal "Papa" Joffre came to an agreement with General Sir Douglas Haig, Commander in Chief of the British Expeditionary Force, to mount a large joint offensive from near Compiègne to the Somme. The French were to engage some forty divisions and the British as many as possible. In fact the French had attacked near Serre in the northern part of the Somme sector in June 1915 and had succeeded in straightening the line. Since then, the Somme front had settled down with a "live and let live" attitude and the Germans had been perfecting their defences to such an extent that they became impregnable fortresses, especially in the north.

The Germans were well aware of the build-up of troops and material on the Western Front and they needed a victory, an outstanding victory, not just to boost the moral of the German people, but also to show to the world the power and invincibility of the German war machine. And so, while the Somme sector was being fortified and held with the minimum number of troops necessary for this purpose, the German high command decided they would break the right wing of the French army by attacking and taking the fortress town of Verdun, the loss of such a prestigious town would surely break French moral. But French patriotism rose to fever-pitch, the nation still retaining bitter memories of the Prussian occupation of Paris only forty six years previously. The Franco-Prussian war must be avenged. Now, Verdun was threatened. Soon the immortal phrases "on ne passera pas", "on les aura" were to become bywords. Not a meter of the sacred soil of France was to be yielded. A young sub-lieutenant at the St. Cyr Military School insisted that there could be no life possible for him in a conquered France and that "Je serai personnellement déshonoré. J'aime mieux beaucoup vivre par mon nom sur une stèle avec la mention, mort au champ d'honneur, que de vivre déshonoré".[Verdun, Jules Romains, page 330, Flammarion, 1938] This translates as "I would be personally disgraced. I would prefer to live through my name on a stone marked 'killed on the field of battle' than to live in disgrace". It was a battle of attrition and more divisions were transferred to Verdun thereby reducing the numbers available for the joint offensive on the Somme. The French would not yield against the German attack and more and more reinforcements had to be sent to replace the terrible losses. The situation was desperate and the French feared the worst. Their casualties at the end of the battle would be over 400,000. The French High Command insisted that the offensive on the Somme must start to relieve the pressure at Verdun. Haig had no choice but to agree although his Third and Fourth Armies were not in the preferred state of readiness - some of the infantry had received minimal training.

It was now very evident that the British would have to bear the brunt of the battle on the Somme and as the long British bombardment began in the last week of June, only five French divisions were assembled in the trenches compared with thirteen British divisions (plus five divisions in reserve). Generals Haig, the C. in C., and Rawlinson in command of the Fourth Army must have been inwardly disappointed but if this was the case no such feelings were relayed to the corps and divisional commanders. The plan of attack had been meticulously prepared; no detail was too small for consideration. In spite of the reduced number of divisions Haig and Rawlinson were optimistic about the effectiveness of the artillery bombardment and were convinced that German opposition would be virtually non-existent. General Allenby G.O.C. of the Third Army at the Gommecourt Diversion did not share this optimism. A large gap between the right flank of his VII Corps and the left flank of the 31st Division attack on Serre would mean his men would inevitably suffer heavy casualties from enfilade fire. Nevertheless, the so-called "Gommecourt Diversion" was destined to go ahead with the aim of drawing German fire away from the Fourth Army attack on the 1st July.

And what of the half million British soldiers? In 1815 Napoléon had contemptuously dismissed his English opponents as "a nation of shopkeepers" but now the descendants of these "shopkeepers" along with bank clerks, miners, railwaymen, builders, university graduates were to fight to defend the soil of France. All the trades and social classes were represented; all had willingly answered Kitchener's call to arms, eager to do their duty for King and Country and the forthcoming battle was, for most of them, to be their baptism of fire. For the working class volunteers it was a chance, not only to do their duty, but to travel and see parts of Europe they could never have hoped to visit in the ordinary course of events. The regular army at the outbreak of war had suffered severe losses at Mons in 1914 and battles mentioned above in 1915. Those who were left were drafted to France with the mass of volunteers, known as the New Army (Service Battalions). There were also the Territorials whose traditional role was to guard the home front but many were posted to the Somme and took part in the attack. One battalion was raised from the farmers, woodcutters and fishermen of Newfoundland, one of our island colonies, and was incorporated into the 29th Division now on the Western Front after its return from Gallipoli. How these erstwhile civilians rose to such heights and performed such deeds of courage on the 1st July reflects both the patriotism and optimism at this time and must rank amongst the very highest disciplined attack in our long military history.

HOW TO USE THIS GUIDE

On the 1st July 1916 a division was composed of three brigades, each brigade having four battalions. In addition each division had one battalion of pioneers. In all, a total of thirteen battalions per division. As a battalion consisted of approximately one thousand men, the divisional commander, with the rank of major-general, had well over thirteen thousand men under his orders. Battalion commanders usually held the rank of lieutenant-colonel. I have not, in the various listings, differentiated between Regular, Territorial or New Army (Service) battalions.

If the reader wishes to trace the steps of a relative and knows in which battalion the soldier served then it is quite easy to trace his path by finding the battalion from the alphabetical list. This will reveal the division, brigade and the sector where he was engaged. The sector is numerically coded and the last section in the guide contains a map, trench list, list of the battalions engaged and a brief description of the action for each sector.

The battalion may be known but not the number. In this case, if it is known where he fought, the battalion can be traced by the coded objective number. The statistics have been listed in different forms to help the reader in his search. It may well be of course, that practically little or no information is known regarding the battalion, brigade or division or where he was engaged. If he died during the battle of the Somme, the Commonwealth War Graves Commission at 2 Marlow Road, Maidenhead, Berkshire, SL6 7DX, will be able to provide information on his regiment, where he is buried or, if the person was listed as missing, on which memorial his name is engraved. It is essential to quote the soldier's serial number. If this is not known but the family has medals awarded to the soldier, the serial number can be found on the outer edge of the General Service Medal and the Victory Medal. On the 1914 Star and the 1914/15 Star, the name and serial number are on the obverse side. If no medals are to hand, the search becomes rather more complicated but not impossible. Let us suppose a reader wishes to trace his ancestor who lived in Warwick at the outbreak of war. It is very possible he enlisted in one of the battalions of the Royal Warwickshire Regiment and initially, contact could be made at the Regimental H.Q. Without a serial number, it is helpful if he did not have the name of Smith, Taylor, Green, etc. but do not be discouraged - he was known to many people. Can you trace any letters or photographs from the soldier to your family or friends? Although it was strictly forbidden to write place names on letters and most were headed B.E.F. France plus the date, it is surprising what passed the censor's scrutiny. It is also very probable he enlisted with some of his friends. Try to make contact with these families as this is one of the best sources of information. Many newly enlisted soldiers had their photograph taken with their friends and many of these pictures are now possibly tucked away in family "archives" throughout the country. It is more than likely he joined the same battalion as his friends. Look at copies of the local newspapers in the archives dated July 1916 or after for information on those who died or were wounded or mentioned in despatches. Articles were abundant on the ordinary soldier. He may not have enlisted in the Warwickshire Regiment at all but perhaps wished to join a kilted regiment or any other whose name or uniform appealed to him. If he survived the war then the chance of finding information more quickly is evidently easier. An advertisement in the local paper may bring some positive result. A further good source of information is the Army Records Office at Hayes in Middlesex. Unfortunately, many records relating to men and women who served in The Great War were destroyed through Luftwaffe bombing during Word War II. However, to give the public greater access to what is still available, they are now transferring the existing records on to microfilm at the Public Records Office at Kew where they can be seen. As soon as you find some information, look at the contents page and you will find the appropriate page number which will advance your research further.

For those readers who are simply on a general visit to the Somme which will probably include a visit to the Newfoundland Park, Thiepval Memorial, Ulster Tower, Lochnagar Crater, Delville Wood and other well-known sites, the guide can be used to find more information from a monument, cemetery or site. For example, on the main Albert-Bapaume road at the approach to the village of La Boisselle, there is the Tyneside Scottish and Irish Memorial seat. From the alphabetical list of battalions with familiar names it will be seen the men were engaged at objective nine. Again turning to the last section of the guide, you will find details of the action in that sector.

It is hoped also that the guide will serve as a source of reference when reading articles on the Somme in newspapers, magazines or books.

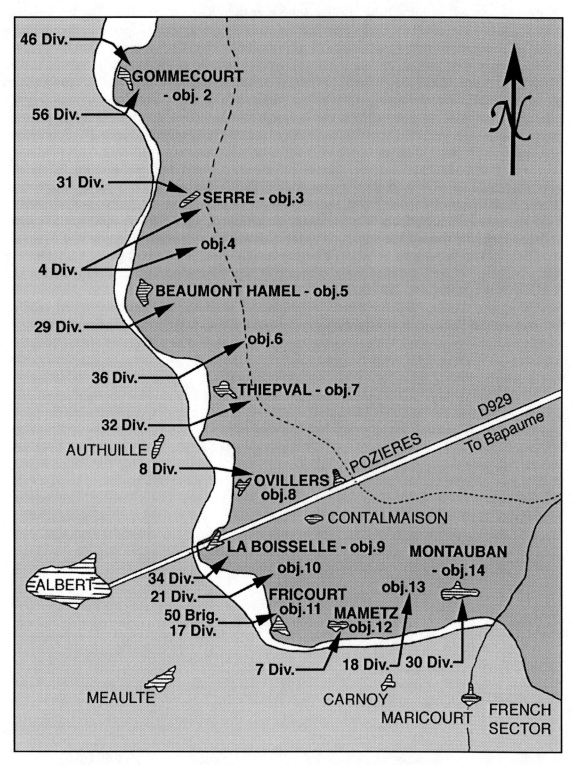

The British positions are on the left, the Germans on the right. The clear zone is 'No Mans Land'.
This is the position at 0730 hrs on 1st July 1916.

OBJECTIVES - 1st JULY, 1916

(The objective code numbers are not official references but numbers allocated by the author to facilitate computer data.)

OBJECT   OBJECTIVE
CODE

0   Battalions in reserve at 7.30am 1st July

1   Not used

2   **THE GOMMECOURT DIVERSION**

        The diversionary attack on the Gommecourt Salient at the extreme north of the British front line on the 1st July was conceived to detract German artillery fire from the left wing of the Fourth Army's attack on Serre, four kilometers to the south east.

3   **SERRE**

        The aim was to take Serre and then pivot on a wide arc to protect the British Divisions to the south and then turn and roll up the German lines from the high ridges north of Beaumont Hamel.

4   **SOUTH OF SERRE AND NORTH OF BEAUMONT HAMEL, THE SERRE-GRANDCOURT RIDGE**

        This attack was planned to help the assault on Serre by taking the Quadrilateral on the left and securing the ridges mentioned above, thereby assisting the important attack on Beaumont Hamel.

5   **BEAUMONT HAMEL, Y RAVINE AND HAWTHORNE RIDGE**

        An attack on an area where the Germans had excellent artillery vision with the obstacles of Hawthorne Ridge and Y Ravine to be taken before the assault on the fortified village of Beaumont Hamel, one of the key German positions.

6   **THE SCHWABEN REDOUBT, ST. PIERRE DIVION AND BEAUCOURT STATION**

        The attack against the Schwaben Redoubt, undoubtedly the strongest of the German fortifications situated on the high ground of Thiepval Ridge. The fortified small village of St. Pierre Divion needed to be neutralised to ensure success of objectives 5 and 6. The German defences at Beaucourt Station also presented potential difficulties for the right wing of objective 5.

7   **THIEPVAL, THE LEIPZIG REDOUBT AND MOUQUET FARM**

        This was the key position to any successful attempt to roll back the German line. With excellent views on all sides, the guardian of Thiepval village and Ridge would have many advantages over any attacking force. The Leipzig Redoubt and its Salient protected Thiepval from the south. Mouquet Farm was a fortress guarding the approach to Pozières and Ovillers.

8   OVILLERS
The capture of this village on the north of the main road would open the way to Pozières, the gateway to Bapaume on the main Amiens/Albert/Cambrai road.

9   LA BOISSELLE AND CONTALMAISON
The capture of La Boisselle just south of the Albert/Bapaume road would clear the main road after the taking of Ovillers and also open the way to the high ground of Fricourt Ridge. The fall of Contalmaison offered access to Mametz Wood and the Bazentin Ridge.

10   THE ATTACK FROM THE SOUTH WEST TOWARDS FRICOURT
The assault was designed to break German communications on the main road from Fricourt to Contalmaison. Birch Tree Wood and Shelter Wood, as well as the large Fricourt Wood on the immediate north east of the village were amongst the objectives. A little further south the capture of Fricourt Farm, Lozenge Wood and Lonely Copse would complete the left wing of a pincer movement to isolate Fricourt.

11   THE ATTACK FROM THE WEST ON FRICOURT VILLAGE
Lying at the point of the British front line where it turns in an easterly direction, Fricourt formed a dangerous salient which needed to be neutralised.

12   MAMETZ AND POMMIERS REDOUBT
The village of Mametz was strongly fortified with Pommiers Redoubt to the east. The taking of both the village and redoubt was essential to straighten the line between Fricourt and Montauban. The left wing of the assault would complete the pincer movement to isolate Fricourt.

13   THE ATTACK EAST OF MAMETZ AND WEST OF MONTAUBAN
This area of open ground contained a number of strong German positions, which, if not taken, would certainly present difficulties to the division designated to take the village of Montauban.

14   MONTAUBAN
This was an important village on the extreme right of the British front line where it linked up with the XX Corps of the French Army.

SENIOR COMMANDERS

COMMANDER IN CHIEF: GENERAL SIR DOUGLAS HAIG

THIRD ARMY: GENERAL SIR E. ALLENBY

VII CORPS: Lieutenant-General Sir T. D'O Snow

		OBJECTIVE No.
46th (North Midland Div.)	Major-General the Hon. E. J. Montagu-Stuart-Wortley	2
56th (London) Division	Major-General C. P. A. Hull	2

FOURTH ARMY: GENERAL SIR H. RAWLINSON

VIII CORPS: Lieutenant-General Sir A. G. Hunter-Weston

31st Division	Maj-Gen. R. Wanless O'Gowan	3
4th Division	Maj-Gen. the Hon. W. Lambton	4
29th Division	Maj-Gen. H. de B. de Lisle	5
48th (South Midland) Div.	Maj-Gen. R. Fanshawe	Reserve (except 6&8/R Wars)

X CORPS: Lieutenant-General Sir T. L. N. Morland

36th (Ulster) Division	Maj-Gen. O. S. W. Nugent	6
32nd Division	Maj-Gen. W. H. Rycroft	7
49th (West Riding) Div.	Maj-Gen. E. M. Perceval	Reserve

III CORPS: Lieutenant-General Sir W. P. Pulteney

8th Division	Maj-Gen. H. Hudson	8
34th Division	Maj-Gen. E. C. Ingouville-Williams	9
19th (Western) Division	Maj-Gen. G. T. M. Bridges	Reserve

XV CORPS: Lieutenant-General H. S. Horne

21st Division	Maj-Gen. D. G. M. Campbell	10
17th (Northern) Division	Maj-Gen. T. D. Pilcher	11
7th Division	Maj-Gen. H. E. Watts	12

XIII CORPS: Lieutenant-General W. N. Congreve V.C.

18th (Eastern) Division	Maj-Gen. F. I. Maxse	13
30th Division	Maj-Gen. J. S. M. Shea	14
9th (Scottish) Division	Maj-Gen. W. T. Furse	Reserve

Disposition of Divisions

Div.	Brig.	No.	Battalion	Obj.
4	10	1	Royal Irish Fusiliers	4
4	10	2	Royal Dublin Fusiliers	4
4	10	2	Seaforth Highlanders	4
4	10	1	Royal Warwicks	4
4	11	1	Somerset Light Infantry	4
4	11	1	East Lancs	4
4	143	8	Royal Warwicks - attached from 48th Div.	4
4	11	1	Hampshires	4
4	11	1	Rifle Brigade	4
4	12	1	King's Own	4
4	12	2	Lancs Fusiliers	4
4	12	2	Duke of Wellington's	4
4	12	2	Essex	4
4	0	21	West Yorks (pioneers)	4
4	143	6	Royal Warwicks - attached from 48th Div.	4
7	20	8	Devons	12
7	20	9	Devons	12
7	20	2	Border	12
7	20	2	Gordon Highlanders	12
7	22	2	Royal Warwicks	12
7	22	20	Manchesters - 5th Manchester Pals	12
7	22	1	Royal Welsh Fusiliers	12
7	22	2	Royal Irish	12
7	91	2	Queen's	12
7	91	1	South Staffs	12
7	91	21	Manchesters - 6th Manchester Pals	12
7	91	22	Manchesters - 7th Manchester Pals	12
7	0	24	Manchesters - Oldham Pals (pioneers)	12
8	23	2	Devons	8
8	23	2	Middlesex	8
8	23	2	West Yorks	8
8	23	2	Scottish Rifles	8
8	25	2	Lincolns	8
8	25	2	Royal Berks	8
8	25	1	Royal Irish Rifles	8
8	25	2	Rifle Brigade	8
8	70	11	Sherwood Foresters - attached to 8th Div. from 23rd	8
8	70	8	King's Own Yorks - attached to 8th Div. from 23rd	8
8	70	8	Yorks and Lancs - attached to 8th Div. from 23rd	8
8	70	9	Yorks and Lancs - attached to 8th Div. from 23rd	8
8	0	22	Durham Light Infantry (Pioneers)	8
9	0	9	Scottish Div - in reserve at 7.30am	0
17	50	10	West Yorks	11
17	50	7	East Yorks	11
17	50	7	Green Howards	11
17	50	6	Dorsets	11
17	51	7	Lincolns (in reserve)	0

Div.	Brig.	No.	Battalion	Obj.
17	51	7	Border (in reserve)	0
17	51	8	South Staffs (in reserve)	0
17	51	10	Sherwood Foresters (in reserve)	0
17	52	9	Northumberland Fusiliers (in reserve)	0
17	52	10	Lancs Fusiliers (in reserve)	0
17	52	9	Duke of Wellington's (in reserve)	0
17	52	12	Manchesters (in reserve)	0
17	0	7	Yorks and Lancs (pioneers)	11
18	53	8	Norfolks	13
18	53	6	Royal Berks	13
18	53	10	Essex	13
18	53	8	Suffolks	13
18	54	11	Royal Fusiliers	13
18	54	7	Bedfords	13
18	54	6	Northamptons	13
18	54	12	Middlesex	13
18	55	7	Queen's	13
18	55	7	Buffs	13
18	55	8	East Surreys	13
18	55	7	Royal West Kents	13
18	0	8	Royal Sussex (pioneers)	13
19	56	7	King's Own - in reserve	0
19	56	7	East Lancs - in reserve	0
19	56	7	South Lancs - in reserve	0
19	56	7	Loyal North Lancs - in reserve	0
19	57	10	Royal Warwicks - in reserve	0
19	57	8	Gloucesters - in reserve	0
19	57	10	Worcesters - in reserve	0
19	57	8	North Staffs - in reserve	0
19	58	9	Cheshires - in reserve	0
19	58	9	Royal Welsh Fusiliers - in reserve	0
19	58	9	Welsh - in reserve	0
19	58	6	Wilts - in reserve	0
19	0	5	South Wales Borderers (pioneers)	0
21	62	12	Northumberland Fusiliers	10
21	62	13	Northumberland Fusiliers	10
21	62	1	Lincolns	10
21	62	10	Green Howards	10
21	63	8	Lincolns	10
21	63	8	Somerset Light Infantry	10
21	63	4	Middlesex	10
21	63	10	Yorks and Lancs	10
21	64	9	King's Own Yorkshire Light Infantry	10
21	64	10	King's Own Yorkshire Light Infantry	10
21	64	1	East Yorks	10
21	64	15	Durham Light Infantry	10
21	0	14	Northumberland Fusiliers (pioneers)	10
29	86	2	Royal Fusiliers	5
29	86	1	Lancs Fusiliers	5

Div.	Brig.	No.	Battalion	Obj.
29	86	16	Middlesex - Public Schools Battalion	5
29	86	1	Royal Dublin Fusiliers	5
29	87	2	South Wales Borderers	5
29	87	1	King's Own Scottish Borderers	5
29	87	1	Royal Inniskilling Fusiliers	5
29	87	1	Border	5
29	88	1	Essex	5
29	88	1	Newfoundland	5
29	88	4	Worcesters	5
29	88	2	Hampshires	5
29	0	2	Monmouths (pioneers)	5
30	21	18	King's - 2nd Liverpool Pals	14
30	21	19	Manchesters - 4th Manchester Pals	14
30	21	2	Wilts	14
30	21	2	Green Howards	14
30	89	17	King's - 1st Liverpool Pals	14
30	89	19	King's - 3rd Liverpool Pals	14
30	89	20	King's - 4th Liverpool Pals	14
30	89	2	Bedfords	14
30	90	2	Royal Scots Fusiliers	14
30	90	16	Manchesters - 1st Manchester Pals	14
30	90	17	Manchesters - 2nd Manchester Pals	14
30	90	18	Manchesters - 3rd Manchester Pals	14
30	0	11	South Lancs (pioneers)	14
31	92	10	East Yorks - Hull Commercials	3
31	92	11	East Yorks - Hull Tradesmen	3
31	92	12	East Yorks - Hull Sportsmen	3
31	92	13	East Yorks - T'Others	3
31	93	15	West Yorks - Leeds Pals	3
31	93	16	West Yorks - 1st Bradford Pals	3
31	93	18	West Yorks - 2nd Bradford Pals	3
31	93	18	Durham Light Infantry - Durham Pals	3
31	94	11	East Lancs - Accrington Pals	3
31	94	12	Yorks and Lancs - Sheffield City Battalion	3
31	94	13	Yorks and Lancs - 1st Barnsley Pals	3
31	94	14	Yorks and Lancs - 2nd Barnsley Pals	3
31	0	12	King's Own Yorks Light Infantry - Halifax Pals (pioneers)	3
32	14	19	Lancs Fusiliers - 3rd Salford Pals	7
32	14	1	Dorsets	7
32	14	2	Manchesters	7
32	14	15	Highland Light Infantry - Glasgow Tramways	7
32	96	16	Northumberland Fusiliers - Newcastle Commercials	7
32	96	2	Royal Inniskilling Fusiliers	7
32	96	15	Lancs Fusiliers - 1st Salford Pals	7
32	96	16	Lancs Fusiliers - 2nd Salford Pals	7
32	97	11	Border, The Lonsdales	7
32	97	2	King's Own Yorkshire Light Infantry	7
32	97	16	Highland Light Infantry - Glasgow Boys Brigade	7
32	97	17	Highland Light Infantry - Glasgow Commercials	7

Div.	Brig.	No.	Battalion	Obj.
32	0	17	Northumberland Fusiliers - Newcastle Railway Pals (pioneers)	7
34	101	15	Royal Scots - 1st Edinburgh City	9
34	101	16	Royal Scots - 2nd Edinburgh City	9
34	101	10	Lincolns - Grimsby Chums	9
34	101	11	Suffolks - Cambridge	9
34	102	20	Northumberland Fusiliers - 1st Tyneside Scottish	9
34	102	21	Northumberland Fusiliers - 2nd Tyneside Scottish	9
34	102	22	Northumberland Fusiliers - 3rd Tyneside Scottish	9
34	102	23	Northumberland Fusiliers - 4th Tyneside Scottish	9
34	103	24	Northumberland Fusiliers - 1st Tyneside Irish	9
34	103	25	Northumberland Fusiliers - 2nd Tyneside Irish	9
34	103	26	Northumberland Fusiliers - 3rd Tyneside Irish	9
34	103	27	Northumberland Fusiliers - 4th Tyneside Irish	9
34	0	18	Northumberland Fusiliers (pioneers)	9
36	107	8	Royal Irish Rifles (E. Belfast)	6
36	107	9	Royal Irish Rifles (W. Belfast)	6
36	107	10	Royal Irish Rifles (S. Belfast)	6
36	107	15	Royal Irish Rifles (N. Belfast)	6
36	108	11	Royal Irish Rifles (S. Antrim)	6
36	108	12	Royal Irish Rifles (Cen. Antrim)	6
36	108	13	Royal Irish Rifles (Co. Down)	6
36	108	9	Royal Irish Fusiliers (Co.Armagh, Monaghan & Cavan)	6
36	109	9	Royal Inniskilling Fusiliers (Co. Tyrone)	6
36	109	10	Royal Inniskilling Fusiliers (Co. Derry)	6
36	109	11	Royal Inniskilling Fusiliers - Donegal & Fermanagh	6
36	109	14	Royal Irish Rifles - Belfast Young Citizens	6
36	0	16	Royal Irish Rifles - 2nd Co. Down (pioneers)	6
37	0	0	All battalions in reserve at 7.30am 1st July	0
46	137	5	South Staffs	2
46	137	6	South Staffs	2
46	137	5	North Staffs	2
46	137	6	North Staffs	2
46	138	4	Lincolns	2
46	138	5	Lincolns	2
46	138	4	Leicesters	2
46	138	5	Leicesters	2
46	139	5	Sherwood Foresters	2
46	139	6	Sherwood Foresters	2
46	139	7	Sherwood Foresters, Robin Hood Rifles	2
46	139	8	Sherwood Foresters	2
46	0	1	Monmouths (pioneers)	2
48	143	5	Royal Warwicks (in reserve)	0
48	143	7	Royal Warwicks (in reserve)	0
48	144	4	Gloucesters (in reserve)	0
48	144	6	Gloucesters (in reserve)	0
48	144	7	Worcesters (in reserve)	0
48	144	8	Worcesters (in reserve)	0
48	145	5	Gloucesters (in reserve)	0
48	145	4	Oxford and Bucks Light Infantry (in reserve)	0

Div.	Brig.	No.	Battalion	Obj.
48	145	1	Bucks (in reserve)	0
48	145	4	Royal Berks (in reserve)	0
48	0	5	Royal Sussex (pioneers)	0
49	146	5	West Yorks (in reserve)	0
49	146	6	West Yorks (in reserve)	0
49	146	7	West Yorks (in reserve)	0
49	146	8	West Yorks (in reserve)	0
49	147	4	Duke of Wellington's (in reserve)	0
49	147	5	Duke of Wellington's (in reserve)	0
49	147	6	Duke of Wellington's (in reserve)	0
49	147	7	Duke of Wellington's (in reserve)	0
49	148	4	Yorks and Lancs (in reserve)	0
49	148	5	Yorks and Lancs (in reserve)	0
49	148	4	King's Own Yorkshire Light Infantry (in reserve)	0
49	148	5	King's Own Yorkshire Light Infantry (in reserve)	0
49	0	3	Monmouths (pioneers)	0
56	167	1	London	2
56	167	3	London	2
56	167	7	Middlesex	2
56	167	8	Middlesex	2
56	168	4	London	2
56	168	12	London - Rangers	2
56	168	13	London - Kensington	2
56	168	14	London - 1st London Scottish	2
56	169	2	London	2
56	169	5	London - 1st London Rifle Brigade	2
56	169	9	London - Queen Victoria's Rifles	2
56	169	16	London - Queen's Westminster Rifles	2
56	0	5	Cheshires (pioneers)	2

Disposition of Brigades

Brig.	Div.	No.	Battalion	Obj.
0	4	21	West Yorks (pioneers)	4
0	7	24	Manchesters - Oldham Pals (pioneers)	12
0	8	22	Durham Light Infantry (Pioneers)	8
0	9	9	Scottish Div - in reserve at 7.30am	0
0	17	7	Yorks and Lancs (pioneers)	11
0	18	8	Royal Sussex (pioneers)	13
0	19	5	South Wales Borderers (pioneers)	0
0	21	14	Northumberland Fusiliers (pioneers)	10
0	29	2	Monmouths (pioneers)	5
0	30	11	South Lancs (pioneers)	14
0	31	12	King's Own Yorkshire Light Infantry - Halifax Pals (pioneers)	3
0	32	17	Northumberland Fusiliers -Newcastle Railway Pals (pioneers)	7
0	34	18	Northumberland Fusiliers (pioneers)	9
0	36	16	Royal Irish Rifles - 2nd Co. Down (pioneers)	6
0	37	0	All battalions in reserve at 7.30am 1st July	0
0	46	1	Monmouths (pioneers)	2
0	48	5	Royal Sussex (pioneers)	0
0	49	3	Monmouths (pioneers)	0
0	56	5	Cheshires (pioneers)	2
10	4	1	Royal Irish Fusiliers	4
10	4	2	Royal Dublin Fusiliers	4
10	4	2	Seaforth Highlanders	4
10	4	1	Royal Warwicks	4
11	4	1	Somerset Light Infantry	4
11	4	1	East Lancs	4
11	4	1	Hampshires	4
11	4	1	Rifle Brigade	4
12	4	1	King's Own	4
12	4	2	Lancs Fusiliers	4
12	4	2	Duke of Wellington's	4
12	4	2	Essex	4
14	32	19	Lancs Fusiliers - 3rd Salford Pals	7
14	32	1	Dorsets	7
14	32	2	Manchesters	7
14	32	15	Highland Light Infantry - Glasgow Tramways	7
20	7	8	Devons	12
20	7	9	Devons	12
20	7	2	Border	12
20	7	2	Gordon Highlanders	12
21	30	18	King's - 2nd Liverpool Pals	14
21	30	19	Manchesters - 4th Manchester Pals	14
21	30	2	Wilts	14
21	30	2	Green Howards	14
22	7	2	Royal Warwicks	12
22	7	20	Manchesters - 5th Manchester Pals	12
22	7	1	Royal Welsh Fusiliers	12
22	7	2	Royal Irish	12

Brig.	Div.	No.	Battalion	Obj.
23	8	2	Devons	8
23	8	2	Middlesex	8
23	8	2	West Yorks	8
23	8	2	Scottish Rifles	8
25	8	2	Lincolns	8
25	8	2	Royal Berks	8
25	8	1	Royal Irish Rifles	8
25	8	2	Rifle Brigade	8
50	17	10	West Yorks	11
50	17	7	East Yorks	11
50	17	7	Green Howards	11
50	17	6	Dorsets	11
51	17	7	Lincolns (in reserve)	0
51	17	7	Border (in reserve)	0
51	17	8	South Staffs (in reserve)	0
51	17	10	Sherwood Foresters (in reserve)	0
52	17	9	Northumberland Fusiliers (in reserve)	0
52	17	10	Lancs Fusiliers (in reserve)	0
52	17	9	Duke of Wellington's (in reserve)	0
52	17	12	Manchesters (in reserve)	0
53	18	8	Norfolks	13
53	18	6	Royal Berks	13
53	18	10	Essex	13
53	18	8	Suffolks	13
54	18	11	Royal Fusiliers	13
54	18	7	Bedfords	13
54	18	6	Northamptons	13
54	18	12	Middlesex	13
55	18	7	Queen's	13
55	18	7	Buffs	13
55	18	8	East Surreys	13
55	18	7	Royal West Kents	13
56	19	7	King's Own - in reserve	0
56	19	7	East Lancs - in reserve	0
56	19	7	South Lancs - in reserve	0
56	19	7	Loyal North Lancs - in reserve	0
57	19	10	Royal Warwicks - in reserve	0
57	19	8	Gloucesters - in reserve	0
57	19	10	Worcesters - in reserve	0
57	19	8	North Staffs - in reserve	0
58	19	9	Cheshires - in reserve	0
58	19	9	Royal Welsh Fusiliers - in reserve	0
58	19	9	Welsh - in reserve	0
58	19	6	Wilts - in reserve	0
62	21	12	Northumberland Fusiliers	10
62	21	13	Northumberland Fusiliers	10
62	21	1	Lincolns	10
62	21	10	Green Howards	10
63	21	8	Lincolns	10

Brig.	Div.	No.	Battalion	Obj.
63	21	8	Somerset Light Infantry	10
63	21	4	Middlesex	10
63	21	10	Yorks and Lancs	10
64	21	9	King's Own Yorkshire Light Infantry	10
64	21	10	King's Own Yorkshire Light Infantry	10
64	21	1	East Yorks	10
64	21	15	Durham Light Infantry	10
70	8	11	Sherwood Foresters - attached to 8th Div. from 23rd	8
70	8	8	King's Own Yorks - attached to 8th Div. from 23rd	8
70	8	8	Yorks and Lancs - attached to 8th Div. from 23rd	8
70	8	9	Yorks and Lancs - attached to 8th Div. from 23rd	8
86	29	2	Royal Fusiliers	5
86	29	1	Lancs Fusiliers	5
86	29	16	Middlesex - Public Schools Battalion	5
86	29	1	Royal Dublin Fusiliers	5
87	29	2	South Wales Borderers	5
87	29	1	King's Own Scottish Borderers	5
87	29	1	Royal Inniskilling Fusiliers	5
87	29	1	Border	5
88	29	1	Essex	5
88	29	1	Newfoundland	5
88	29	4	Worcesters	5
88	29	2	Hampshires	5
89	30	17	King's - 1st Liverpool Pals	14
89	30	19	King's - 3rd Liverpool Pals	14
89	30	20	King's - 4th Liverpool Pals	14
89	30	2	Bedfords	14
90	30	2	Royal Scots Fusiliers	14
90	30	16	Manchesters - 1st Manchester Pals	14
90	30	17	Manchesters - 2nd Manchester Pals	14
90	30	18	Manchesters - 3rd Manchester Pals	14
91	7	2	Queen's	12
91	7	1	South Staffs	12
91	7	21	Manchesters - 6th Manchester Pals	12
91	7	22	Manchesters - 7th Manchester Pals	12
92	31	10	East Yorks - Hull Commercials	3
92	31	11	East Yorks - Hull Tradesmen	3
92	31	12	East Yorks - Hull Sportsmen	3
92	31	13	East Yorks - T'Others	3
93	31	15	West Yorks - Leeds Pals	3
93	31	16	West Yorks - 1st Bradford Pals	3
93	31	18	West Yorks - 2nd Bradford Pals	3
93	31	18	Durham Light Infantry - Durham Pals	3
94	31	11	East Lancs - Accrington Pals	3
94	31	12	Yorks and Lancs - Sheffield City Battalion	3
94	31	13	Yorks and Lancs - 1st Barnsley Pals	3
94	31	14	Yorks and Lancs - 2nd Barnsley Pals	3
96	32	16	Northumberland Fusiliers - Newcastle Commercials	7

Brig.	Div.	No.	Battalion	Obj.
96	32	2	Royal Inniskilling Fusiliers	7
96	32	15	Lancs Fusiliers - 1st Salford Pals	7
96	32	16	Lancs Fusiliers - 2nd Salford Pals	7
97	32	11	Border, The Lonsdales	7
97	32	2	King's Own Yorkshire Light Infantry	7
97	32	16	Highland Light Infantry - Glasgow Boys Brigade	7
97	32	17	Highland Light Infantry - Glasgow Commercials	7
101	34	15	Royal Scots - 1st Edinburgh City	9
101	34	16	Royal Scots - 2nd Edinburgh City	9
101	34	10	Lincolns - Grimsby Chums	9
101	34	11	Suffolks - Cambridge	9
102	34	20	Northumberland Fusiliers - 1st Tyneside Scottish	9
102	34	21	Northumberland Fusiliers - 2nd Tyneside Scottish	9
102	34	22	Northumberland Fusiliers - 3rd Tyneside Scottish	9
102	34	23	Northumberland Fusiliers - 4th Tyneside Scottish	9
103	34	24	Northumberland Fusiliers - 1st Tyneside Irish	9
103	34	25	Northumberland Fusiliers - 2nd Tyneside Irish	9
103	34	26	Northumberland Fusiliers - 3rd Tyneside Irish	9
103	34	27	Northumberland Fusiliers - 4th Tyneside Irish	9
107	36	8	Royal Irish Rifles (E. Belfast)	6
107	36	9	Royal Irish Rifles (W. Belfast)	6
107	36	10	Royal Irish Rifles (S. Belfast)	6
107	36	15	Royal Irish Rifles (N. Belfast)	6
108	36	11	Royal Irish Rifles (S. Antrim)	6
108	36	12	Royal Irish Rifles (Cen. Antrim)	6
108	36	13	Royal Irish Rifles (Co. Down)	6
108	36	9	Royal Irish Fusiliers (Co. Armagh, Monaghan & Cavan)	6
109	36	9	Royal Inniskilling Fusiliers (Co. Tyrone)	6
109	36	10	Royal Inniskilling Fusiliers (Co. Derry)	6
109	36	11	Royal Inniskilling Fusiliers - Donegal & Fermanagh	6
109	36	14	Royal Irish Rifles - Belfast Young Citizens	6
137	46	5	South Staffs	2
137	46	6	South Staffs	2
137	46	5	North Staffs	2
137	46	6	North Staffs	2
138	46	4	Lincolns	2
138	46	5	Lincolns	2
138	46	4	Leicesters	2
138	46	5	Leicesters	2
139	46	5	Sherwood Foresters	2
139	46	6	Sherwood Foresters	2
139	46	7	Sherwood Foresters, Robin Hood Rifles	2
139	46	8	Sherwood Foresters	2
143	4	8	Royal Warwicks - attached from 48th Div.	4
143	4	6	Royal Warwicks - attached from 48th Div.	4
143	48	5	Royal Warwicks (in reserve)	0
143	48	7	Royal Warwicks (in reserve)	0

Brig.	Div.	No.	Battalion	Obj.
144	48	4	Gloucesters (in reserve)	0
144	48	6	Gloucesters (in reserve)	0
144	48	7	Worcesters (in reserve)	0
144	48	8	Worcesters (in reserve)	0
145	48	5	Gloucesters (in reserve)	0
145	48	4	Oxford and Bucks Light Infantry (in reserve)	0
145	48	1	Bucks (in reserve)	0
145	48	4	Royal Berks (in reserve)	0
146	49	5	West Yorks (in reserve)	0
146	49	6	West Yorks (in reserve)	0
146	49	7	West Yorks (in reserve)	0
146	49	8	West Yorks (in reserve)	0
147	49	4	Duke of Wellington's (in reserve)	0
147	49	5	Duke of Wellington's (in reserve)	0
147	49	6	Duke of Wellington's (in reserve)	0
147	49	7	Duke of Wellington's (in reserve)	0
148	49	4	Yorks and Lancs (in reserve)	0
148	49	5	Yorks and Lancs (in reserve)	0
148	49	4	King's Own Yorkshire Light Infantry (in reserve)	0
148	49	5	King's Own Yorkshire Light Infantry (in reserve)	0
167	56	1	London	2
167	56	3	London	2
167	56	7	Middlesex	2
167	56	8	Middlesex	2
168	56	4	London	2
168	56	12	London - Rangers	2
168	56	13	London - Kensington	2
168	56	14	London - 1st London Scottish	2
169	56	2	London	2
169	56	5	London - 1st London Rifle Brigade	2
169	56	9	London - Queen Victoria's Rifles	2
169	56	16	London - Queen's Westminster Rifles	2

Battalions in alphabetical order

Div.	Brig.	No.	Battalion	Objective
37	0	0	All battalions in reserve at 7.30am 1st July	0
18	54	7	Bedfords	13
30	89	2	Bedfords	14
7	20	2	Border	12
29	87	1	Border	5
17	51	7	Border (in reserve)	0
32	97	11	Border, The Lonsdales	7
48	145	1	Bucks (in reserve)	0
18	55	7	Buffs	13
19	58	9	Cheshires - in reserve	0
56	0	5	Cheshires (pioneers)	2
7	20	8	Devons	12
7	20	9	Devons	12
8	23	2	Devons	8
17	50	6	Dorsets	11
32	14	1	Dorsets	7
4	12	2	Duke of Wellington's	4
17	52	9	Duke of Wellington's (in reserve)	0
49	147	4	Duke of Wellington's (in reserve)	0
49	147	5	Duke of Wellington's (in reserve)	0
49	147	6	Duke of Wellington's (in reserve)	0
49	147	7	Duke of Wellington's (in reserve)	0
21	64	15	Durham Light Infantry	10
8	0	22	Durham Light Infantry (Pioneers)	8
31	93	18	Durham Light Infantry - Durham Pals	3
4	11	1	East Lancs	4
31	94	11	East Lancs - Accrington Pals	3
19	56	7	East Lancs - in reserve	0
18	55	8	East Surreys	13
17	50	7	East Yorks	11
21	64	1	East Yorks	10
31	92	10	East Yorks - Hull Commercials	3
31	92	12	East Yorks - Hull Sportsmen	3
31	92	11	East Yorks - Hull Tradesmen	3
31	92	13	East Yorks - T'Others	3
4	12	2	Essex	4
18	53	10	Essex	13
29	88	1	Essex	5
19	57	8	Gloucesters - in reserve	0
48	144	4	Gloucesters (in reserve)	0
48	144	6	Gloucesters (in reserve)	0
48	145	5	Gloucesters (in reserve)	0
7	20	2	Gordon Highlanders	12
17	50	7	Green Howards	11
21	62	10	Green Howards	10
30	21	2	Green Howards	14
4	11	1	Hampshires	4

Div.	Brig.	No.	Battalion	Obj.
29	88	2	Hampshires	5
32	97	16	Highland Light Infantry - Glasgow Boys Brigade	7
32	14	15	Highland Light Infantry - Glasgow Tramways	7
32	97	17	Highland Light Infantry - Glasgow Commercials	7
30	89	17	King's - 1st Liverpool Pals	14
30	21	18	King's - 2nd Liverpool Pals	14
30	89	19	King's - 3rd Liverpool Pals	14
30	89	20	King's - 4th Liverpool Pals	14
4	12	1	King's Own	4
19	56	7	King's Own - in reserve	0
29	87	1	King's Own Scottish Borderers	5
8	70	8	King's Own Yorks - attached to 8th Div. from 23rd	8
21	64	9	King's Own Yorkshire Light Infantry	10
21	64	10	King's Own Yorkshire Light Infantry	10
32	97	2	King's Own Yorkshire Light Infantry	7
31	0	12	King's Own Yorks Light Infantry - Halifax Pals (pioneers)	3
49	148	4	King's Own Yorkshire Light Infantry (in reserve)	0
49	148	5	King's Own Yorkshire Light Infantry (in reserve)	0
4	12	2	Lancs Fusiliers	4
29	86	1	Lancs Fusiliers	5
32	96	15	Lancs Fusiliers - 1st Salford Pals	7
32	96	16	Lancs Fusiliers - 2nd Salford Pals	7
32	14	19	Lancs Fusiliers - 3rd Salford Pals	7
17	52	10	Lancs Fusiliers (in reserve)	0
46	138	4	Leicesters	2
46	138	5	Leicesters	2
8	25	2	Lincolns	8
21	62	1	Lincolns	10
21	63	8	Lincolns	10
46	138	4	Lincolns	2
46	138	5	Lincolns	2
34	101	10	Lincolns - Grimsby Chums	9
17	51	7	Lincolns (in reserve)	0
56	167	1	London	2
56	167	3	London	2
56	168	4	London	2
56	169	2	London	2
56	169	5	London - 1st London Rifle Brigade	2
56	168	14	London - 1st London Scottish	2
56	168	13	London - Kensington	2
56	169	9	London - Queen Victoria's Rifles	2
56	169	16	London - Queen's Westminster Rifles	2
56	168	12	London - Rangers	2
19	56	7	Loyal North Lancs - in reserve	0
32	14	2	Manchesters	7
30	90	16	Manchesters - 1st Manchester Pals	14
30	90	17	Manchesters - 2nd Manchester Pals	14
30	90	18	Manchesters - 3rd Manchester Pals	14

Div.	Brig.	No.	Battalion	Obj.
30	21	19	Manchesters - 4th Manchester Pals	14
7	22	20	Manchesters - 5th Manchester Pals	12
7	91	21	Manchesters - 6th Manchester Pals	12
7	91	22	Manchesters - 7th Manchester Pals	12
7	0	24	Manchesters - Oldham Pals (pioneers)	12
17	52	12	Manchesters (in reserve)	0
8	23	2	Middlesex	8
18	54	12	Middlesex	13
21	63	4	Middlesex	10
56	167	7	Middlesex	2
56	167	8	Middlesex	2
29	86	16	Middlesex - Public Schools Battalion	5
29	0	2	Monmouths (pioneers)	5
46	0	1	Monmouths (pioneers)	2
49	0	3	Monmouths (pioneers)	0
29	88	1	Newfoundland	5
18	53	8	Norfolks	13
46	137	5	North Staffs	2
46	137	6	North Staffs	2
19	57	8	North Staffs - in reserve	0
18	54	6	Northamptons	13
21	62	12	Northumberland Fusiliers	10
21	62	13	Northumberland Fusiliers	10
34	103	24	Northumberland Fusiliers - 1st Tyneside Irish	9
34	102	20	Northumberland Fusiliers - 1st Tyneside Scottish	9
34	103	25	Northumberland Fusiliers - 2nd Tyneside Irish	9
34	102	21	Northumberland Fusiliers - 2nd Tyneside Scottish	9
34	103	26	Northumberland Fusiliers - 3rd Tyneside Irish	9
34	102	22	Northumberland Fusiliers - 3rd Tyneside Scottish	9
34	103	27	Northumberland Fusiliers - 4th Tyneside Irish	9
34	102	23	Northumberland Fusiliers - 4th Tyneside Scottish	9
32	96	16	Northumberland Fusiliers - Newcastle Commercials	7
32	0	17	Northumberland Fusiliers - Newcastle Railway Pals (pioneers)	7
17	52	9	Northumberland Fusiliers (in reserve)	0
21	0	14	Northumberland Fusiliers (pioneers)	10
34	0	18	Northumberland Fusiliers (pioneers)	9
48	145	4	Oxford and Bucks Light Infantry (in reserve)	0
7	91	2	Queen's	12
18	55	7	Queen's	13
4	11	1	Rifle Brigade	4
8	25	2	Rifle Brigade	8
8	25	2	Royal Berks	8
18	53	6	Royal Berks	13
48	145	4	Royal Berks (in reserve)	0
4	10	2	Royal Dublin Fusiliers	4
29	86	1	Royal Dublin Fusiliers	5
18	54	11	Royal Fusiliers	13
29	86	2	Royal Fusiliers	5
29	87	1	Royal Inniskilling Fusiliers	5

Div.	Brig.	No.	Battalion	Obj.
32	96	2	Royal Inniskilling Fusiliers	7
36	109	11	Royal Inniskilling Fusiliers - Donegal & Fermanagh	6
36	109	10	Royal Inniskilling Fusiliers (Co. Derry)	6
36	109	9	Royal Inniskilling Fusiliers (Co. Tyrone)	6
7	22	2	Royal Irish	12
4	10	1	Royal Irish Fusiliers	4
36	108	9	Royal Irish Fusiliers (Co. Armagh, Monaghan & Cavan)	6
8	25	1	Royal Irish Rifles	8
36	0	16	Royal Irish Rifles - 2nd Co. Down (pioneers)	6
36	109	14	Royal Irish Rifles - Belfast Young Citizens	6
36	108	12	Royal Irish Rifles (Cen. Antrim)	6
36	108	13	Royal Irish Rifles (Co. Down)	6
36	107	8	Royal Irish Rifles (E. Belfast)	6
36	107	15	Royal Irish Rifles (N. Belfast)	6
36	108	11	Royal Irish Rifles (S. Antrim)	6
36	107	10	Royal Irish Rifles (S. Belfast)	6
36	107	9	Royal Irish Rifles (W. Belfast)	6
34	101	15	Royal Scots - 1st Edinburgh City	9
34	101	16	Royal Scots - 2nd Edinburgh City	9
30	90	2	Royal Scots Fusiliers	14
18	0	8	Royal Sussex (pioneers)	13
48	0	5	Royal Sussex (pioneers)	0
4	10	1	Royal Warwicks	4
7	22	2	Royal Warwicks	12
4	143	8	Royal Warwicks - attached from 48th Div.	4
4	143	6	Royal Warwicks - attached from 48th Div.	4
19	57	10	Royal Warwicks - in reserve	0
48	143	5	Royal Warwicks (in reserve)	0
48	143	7	Royal Warwicks (in reserve)	0
7	22	1	Royal Welsh Fusiliers	12
19	58	9	Royal Welsh Fusiliers - in reserve	0
18	55	7	Royal West Kents	13
9	0	9	Scottish Div - in reserve at 7.30am	0
8	23	2	Scottish Rifles	8
4	10	2	Seaforth Highlanders	4
46	139	5	Sherwood Foresters	2
46	139	6	Sherwood Foresters	2
46	139	8	Sherwood Foresters	2
8	70	11	Sherwood Foresters - attached to 8th Div. from 23rd	8
17	51	10	Sherwood Foresters (in reserve)	0
46	139	7	Sherwood Foresters, Robin Hood Rifles	2
4	11	1	Somerset Light Infantry	4
21	63	8	Somerset Light Infantry	10
19	56	7	South Lancs - in reserve	0
30	0	11	South Lancs (pioneers)	14
7	91	1	South Staffs	12
46	137	5	South Staffs	2
46	137	6	South Staffs	2

Div.	Brig.	No.	Battalion	Obj.
17	51	8	South Staffs (in reserve)	0
29	87	2	South Wales Borderers	5
19	0	5	South Wales Borderers (pioneers)	0
18	53	8	Suffolks	13
34	101	11	Suffolks - Cambridge	9
19	58	9	Welsh - in reserve	0
8	23	2	West Yorks	8
17	50	10	West Yorks	11
31	93	16	West Yorks - 1st Bradford Pals	3
31	93	18	West Yorks - 2nd Bradford Pals	3
31	93	15	West Yorks - Leeds Pals	3
49	146	5	West Yorks (in reserve)	0
49	146	6	West Yorks (in reserve)	0
49	146	7	West Yorks (in reserve)	0
49	146	8	West Yorks (in reserve)	0
4	0	21	West Yorks (pioneers)	4
30	21	2	Wilts	14
19	58	6	Wilts - in reserve	0
29	88	4	Worcesters	5
19	57	10	Worcesters - in reserve	0
48	144	7	Worcesters (in reserve)	0
48	144	8	Worcesters (in reserve)	0
21	63	10	Yorks and Lancs	10
31	94	13	Yorks and Lancs - 1st Barnsley Pals	3
31	94	14	Yorks and Lancs - 2nd Barnsley Pals	3
8	70	8	Yorks and Lancs - attached to 8th Div. from 23rd	8
8	70	9	Yorks and Lancs - attached to 8th Div. from 23rd	8
31	94	12	Yorks and Lancs - Sheffield City Battalion	3
49	148	4	Yorks and Lancs (in reserve)	0
49	148	5	Yorks and Lancs (in reserve)	0
17	0	7	Yorks and Lancs (pioneers)	11

Battalions having informal names

Div.	Brig.	Familiar name	Obj
31	94	Accrington Pals - 11th East Lancs	3
31	94	Barnsley Pals (1st) - 13th Yorks and Lancs	3
31	94	Barnsley Pals (2nd) - 14th Yorks and Lancs	3
36	109	Belfast Young Citizens - 14th Royal Irish Rifles	6
31	93	Bradford Pals (1st) - 16th West Yorks	3
31	93	Bradford Pals (2nd) - 18th West Yorks	3
34	101	Cambridge - 11th Suffolks	9
36	108	Central Antrim - 12th Royal Irish Rifles	6
36	108	Co. Armagh, Monaghan & Cavan - 9th Royal Irish Fusiliers	6
36	109	County Derry - 10th Royal Inniskilling Fusiliers	6
36	108	County Down - 13th Royal Irish Rifles	6
36	0	County Down (2nd) - 16th Royal Irish Rifles (Pnrs.)	6
36	109	County Tyrone - 9th Royal Inniskilling Fusiliers	6
36	109	Donegal & Fermanagh - 11th Royal Inniskilling Fusiliers	6
31	93	Durham Pals -18th Durham Light Infantry	3
36	107	East Belfast - 8th Royal Irish Rifles	6
34	101	Edinburgh City (1st) - 15th Royal Scots	9
34	101	Edinburgh City (2nd) - 16th Royal Scots	9
32	97	Glasgow Boys Brigade - 16th Highland Light Infantry	7
32	97	Glasgow Commercials - 17th Highland Light Infantry	7
32	14	Glasgow Tramways - 15th Highland Light Infantry	7
30	21	Green Howards (2nd) - 2nd Yorks	14
21	62	Green Howards (10th) - 10th Yorks	10
17	50	Green Howards (7th) - 7th Yorks	11
34	101	Grimsby Chums - 10th Lincolns	9
31	0	Halifax Pals - 12th K.O.L.I. (Pioneers)	3
31	92	Hull Commercials - 10th East Yorks	3
31	92	Hull Sportsmen - 12th East Yorks	3
31	92	Hull Tradesmen - 11th East Yorks	3
56	168	Kensington - 13th London	2
31	93	Leeds Pals - 15th West Yorks	3
30	89	Liverpool Pals (1st) - 17th King's	14
30	21	Liverpool Pals (2nd) - 18th King's	14
30	89	Liverpool Pals (3rd) - 19th King's	14
30	89	Liverpool Pals (4th)- 2nd King's	14
56	169	London Rifle Brigade (1st) - 5th London	2
56	168	London Scottish (1st) - 14th London	2
32	97	Lonsdales - 11th Border	7
30	90	Manchester Pals (1st) - 16th Manchesters	14
30	90	Manchester Pals (2nd) - 17th Manchesters	14
30	90	Manchester Pals (3rd) - 18th Manchesters	14
30	21	Manchester Pals (4th) - 19th Manchesters	14
7	22	Manchester Pals (5th) - 20th Manchesters	12
7	91	Manchester Pals (6th) - 21st Manchesters	12
7	91	Manchester Pals (7th) - 22nd Manchesters	12

Div.	Brig.	Familiar name	Obj.
32	96	Newcastle Commercials - 16th Northumberland Fusiliers	7
32	0	Newcastle Railway Pals - 17th Northumberland Fusiliers (Pnr)	7
36	107	North Belfast - 15th Royal Irish Rifles	6
7	0	Oldham Pals - 24th Manchesters (Pioneers)	12
29	86	Public Schools Battalion - 16th Middlesex	5
56	169	Queen Victoria's Rifles - 9th London	2
56	169	Queen's Westminster Rifles - 16th London	2
56	168	Rangers - 12th London	2
46	139	Robin Hood Rifles - 7th Sherwood Foresters	2
32	96	Salford Pals (1st) -15th Lancs Fusiliers	7
32	96	Salford Pals (2nd) - 16th Lancs Fusiliers	7
32	14	Salford Pals (3rd) - 19th Lancs Fusiliers	7
31	94	Sheffield City Battalion - 12th Yorks and Lancs	3
36	108	South Antrim - 11th Royal Irish Rifles	6
36	107	South Belfast - 10th Royal Irish Rifles	6
31	92	T'Others - 13th East Yorks	3
34	103	Tyneside Irish (1st) - 24th Northumberland Fusiliers	9
34	103	Tyneside Irish (2nd) - 25th Northumberland Fusiliers	9
34	103	Tyneside Irish (3rd) - 26th Northumberland Fusiliers	9
34	103	Tyneside Irish (4th) - 27th Northumberland Fusiliers	9
34	0	Tyneside Pioneers (1st) - 18th Northumberland Fusiliers	9
34	102	Tyneside Scottish (1st) - 20th Northumberland Fusiliers	9
34	102	Tyneside Scottish (2nd) - 21st Northumberland Fusiliers	9
34	102	Tyneside Scottish (3rd) - 22nd Northumberland Fusiliers	9
34	102	Tyneside Scottish (4th) - 23rd Northumberland Fusiliers	9
36	107	West Belfast - 9th Royal Irish Rifles	6

Battalions in reserve at 07.30hrs, 1st July 1916

Corps.	Div.	Brig.	No.	Battalion
VII	37th	0	0	All battalions in reserve at 7.30am
XV	17th	51st	7th	Border
VIII	48th	145th	1st	Bucks
III	19th	58th	9th	Cheshire
X	49th	147th	4th	Duke of Wellington's
X	49th	147th	5th	Duke of Wellington's
X	49th	147th	6th	Duke of Wellington's
X	49th	147th	7th	Duke of Wellington's
XV	17th	52nd	9th	Duke of Wellington's
III	19th	56th	7th	East Lancs
VIII	48th	144th	4th	Gloucester
VIII	48th	144th	6th	Gloucester
VIII	48th	145th	5th	Gloucester
III	19th	57th	8th	Gloucester
III	19th	56th	7th	King's Own
X	49th	148th	4th	K.O.Y.L.I.
X	49th	148th	5th	K.O.Y.L.I.
XV	17th	52nd	10th	Lancs Fusiliers
XV	17th	51st	7th	Lincoln
III	19th	56th	7th	Loyal North Lancs
XV	17th	52nd	12th	Manchester
X	49th	0	3rd	Monmouths - pioneers
III	19th	57th	8th	North Staffs
XV	17th	52nd	9th	Northumberland Fusiliers
VIII	48th	145th	4th	Oxford & Bucks Light Infantry
VIII	48th	145th	4th	Royal Berks
VIII	48th	0	5th	Royal Sussex - pioneers
VIII	48th	143rd	5th	Royal Warwick
VIII	48th	143rd	6th	Royal Warwick
VIII	48th	143rd	7th	Royal Warwick
VIII	48th	143rd	8th	Royal Warwick
III	19th	57th	10th	Royal Warwick
III	19th	58th	9th	Royal Welsh Fusiliers
XIII	9th	0		All battalions in reserve
XV	17th	51st	10th	Sherwood Foresters
III	19th	56th	7th	South Lancs
XV	17th	51st	8th	South Staffs
III	19th	0	5th	South Wales Borderers - pioneers
III	19th	58th	9th	Welsh
X	49th	146th	5th	West Yorks
X	49th	146th	6th	West Yorks
X	49th	146th	7th	West Yorks

Corps.	Div.	Brig.	No.	Battalion
X	49th	146th	8th	West Yorks
III	19th	58th	6th	Wilts
VIII	48th	144th	7th	Worcester
VIII	48th	144th	8th	Worcester
III	19th	57th	10th	Worcester
X	49th	148th	4th	Yorks & Lancs
X	49th	148th	5th	Yorks & Lancs

THE I.G.N. MAPS
AND REFERENCE NUMBERS

Four I.G.N. (Institut Géographique National) maps on a scale of 1:25 000, i.e. 4cm = 1km or 694.4 yards = one inch cover the whole of the battle area from the 1st July to mid-November when the campaign became bogged down in severe wet conditions.

2407 Ouest (West) which is shown simply as 7 W on the lists			
2408 Est (East)	"	8 E	"
2407 Est (East)	"	7 E	"
2408 Ouest (West)	"	8 W	"

Of these maps the first two cover the events of the 1st July. They are readily available from the two main stationers in the town of Albert in the Somme. At the time of writing the cost was 46 French francs each. If you are well out of the Somme area, the maps may have to be ordered. In England, they can be ordered from a number of large booksellers. I have always liked these large-scale maps with so much detail; many are the small bitterly contested quarries to be found on these maps.

The map references quoted on lists have been done in the traditional way, i.e. Eastings followed by Northings. Most references refer to a one kilometer square, but a number of trenches have been given references to one hundred metres and, in a few cases to an accuracy of 50 metres. The reference numbers on the maps are shown in two colours, black and blue. ALL the references quoted on the lists are taken from the BLUE figures (known as the Lambert Zone Two). Personally, I have ruled the maps into one kilometer squares (always with the blue figures) and I find this extremely useful - the references can be found in an instant on the appropriate map.

A number of references have been given a + sign after the eastings or northings reference, e.g: from page 53: 621+/2564 means that St John's Road extends EAST outside the kilometer square 621/2564. Similarly, also from page 53: 623/2565+ means that Ten Tree Alley extends NORTH outside the kilometer square 623/2565.

When the maps of the first world war were being compiled for the army, some changes were made to the names of certain sites and the Bois d'Authuille, just west of Thiepval is always cited as Thiepval Wood on British military maps of the period. Similarly, the Bois de la Haie is known as Authuille Wood. All references in this guide to these woods use the English names found on British trench maps. Some interesting transpositional errors were made by cartographers and the village of Foncquevillers at the northern end of the line is often listed on British maps as Fonquevillers and the Bois des Troncs, first attacked on the 8th July and finally taken a week later, is always shown on British maps as Trones Wood. It would not have been wise to officially change the names of villages and so the men had to cope with some strange names and very quickly, Auchonvillers became known as "Ocean Villas" to the men and other places took rather odd names when Anglicized.

Trenches, battle sites, etc. in alphabetical order

Site / Trench	Location	Map	Map Ref.	Obj.
1st Avenue	W of Y Ravine	7 W	622/2564	5
2nd Avenue	S of 3rd Av on old Beaumont Rd.	7 W	621/2565	5
3rd Avenue	Runs SW from White City	7 W	621/2565	5
4th Avenue	NW of Pozières	7 E	627+/2561	7
4th Avenue	Just S of 5th Avenue	7 W	621/2565	5
5th Avenue	W of Leipzig Salient	7 W	624/2561	7
5th Avenue	Runs W from White City	7 W	621/2565	5
88 T	Cont. S of Lunar Trench	7 W	622/2564+	5
88th Trench	Hawthorne Ridge	7 W	622/2564+	5
Abeyne Street	ESE of Chapes Spur	8 W	625/2557	9
Acid Drop Copse	420m ESE of Contalmaison	8 E	626/2558	10
Aeroplane Trench	1300m W of Mametz Halt	8 E	627/2555	12
Aintree Street	Authuille Wood	7 W	624/2559+	8
Alt Trench	SE from Train Alley	8 E	631/2555	14
Alte Jager Stellung	800m E of La Boisselle	8 E	626/2558	9
Ancre Trench	Runs E from Beaucourt	7 W	625/2565	5
Andrews Avenue	Nr. Keats Redan	8 W	624/2558	8
Anna (pioneer trench)	420m WNW of Rossignol Wood	7 W	623/2570	2
Anstruther Street	SE of Ovillers Post	8 W	624/2558	8
Ant Trench	560m WSW of Rossignol Wood	7 W	623/2570	2
Apple Alley	600m W of Mametz Halt	8 E	627/2555	12
Aragon Trench	1100M SE of Rossignol Wood	7 W	624/2569	2
Arbroath Street	Just N of Chapes Spur	8 W	625/2557	9
Ardgour Street	Just E of Authuille village	7 W	624/2560	7
Ardnshaig Street	Just E of Authuille village	7 W	624/2560	7
Argyll Street	700m E of Ovillers Post	8 W	625/2558	8
Arrow Lane	Just N of Lonely Lane	8 E	627/2556	11
Arthur Street	E of Thiepval Wood	7 W	624/2561+	7
Artillery Lane	NNW of Beaucourt sur Ancre	7 W	624/2565	5
Arun Trench	470m S of Rossignol Wood	7 W	624/2570	2
Ashtown Street	Just N of Chapes Spur	8 W	625/2557	9
Athall Street	NNW of Chapes Spur	8 W	625/2557	9
Austrian Junction	E off S end of Back Alley	8 E	629/2556	13
Austrian Trench	S of Austrian Junction	8 E	629/2556	13
Authuille Bridge	over Ancre NW Authuille	7 W	623/2560	7
Authuille Wood	Assy of 70th Brig. for 1 July attack	8 W	624/2559+	7
Avoca Valley	Between Tara Hill & Bécourt	8 W	624/2556	9
Babylon	N from Observation Wood	7 W	621/2567	3
Back Alley	1300m NNW of Carnoy	8 E	629/2556	13
Back Lane	S of Breslau Alley	8 E	631/2555	13
Back Trench	240m N of Breslau Trench	8 E	631/2555	13
Baillescourt Farm	540m NNW of Grandcourt centre	7 E	6267/25656	5
Ball Lane	Joins Lozenge Alley from W	8 E	626/2556	10
Barlow Street	Just W of Ovillers	8 W	625/2559	8

Site / Trench	Location	Map	Map Ref.	Obj.
Barrow Road	Near Ovillers	8 E	626/2559	8
Basin Wood	CCS & Mass burial site			
	nr.La Signy Farm	7 W	621/2567	3
Battalion Trench	E of Hawthorne Crater	7 W	622/2565	5
Battery Valley	1600m NE of Schwaben Redoubt	7 W	624/2562+	7
Bay Trench	Contn. of E of Emden Trench	8 E	630/2556	13
Beaucourt Mill	800m SSW of Beaucourt	7 W	624/2564	5
Beaucourt Redoubt	350m NW of Beaucourt	7 W	624/2565	7
Beaucourt sur l'Ancre	2000m E Beaumont Hamel	7 W	625/2564	5
Beaumont Alley	E exit from Beaumont Hamel	7 W	623/2565	5
Beaumont Hamel	1500m SE of			
Station	Beaumont Hamel	7 W	624/2564	5
Beaumont Hamel	2000m E Auchonvillers	7 W	623/2565	5
Beaumont Trench	Near Redan Ridge	7 W	623+/2564+	5
Bécourt Avenue	Comm. T. crossing Tara Hill	8 W	624/2557	9
Bergwerk	Just N of Beaumont Hamel	7 W	623/2565	5
Berkshire Avenue	Comm. T Albert to Avoca Valley	8 W	623+/2556	9
Birch Tree Trench	NE from Birch Tree Wood	8 E	627/2557	11
Bisset Trench	Just W of Leipzig Salient	7 W	624/2561	7
Black Alley	600m SSW of Pommiers Redoubt	8 E	629/2555	13
Black Hedge	900m SSW of Pommiers Redoubt	8 E	629/2555	13
Black Horse Bridge	Bridge SSW of Authuille	7 W	623/2560	7
Black Horse Road	Just SW of Authuille	7 W	623/2560	7
Black Trench	W of Black Hedge	8 E	629/2555	12
Blackfriars Bridge	Bridge over trenches at Serre	7 W	622/2567	3
Blind Alley	800m E of Pommiers Redoubt	8 E	630/2556	13
Bloater Trench	500m E of Lochnagar crater	8 E	626/2558	10
Bloomfield Avenue	Runs W from S of Rough Trench	7 W	622/2565	5
Boche Trench	Just S of The Loop	8 E	630/2555	13
Bois de Biez	E of Gommecourt Park	7 W	624/2571	2
Bois d'Hollande	NE of Beaucourt	7 E	626/2565	5
Bois du Sartel (see				
Gommecourt Wd)	SW of Foncquevillers	7 W	622/2571+	2
Boisselle Street	400m E of Ovillers Post	8 W	624/2558	8
Bond Street	S of Y Ravine	7 W	622/2564	5
Bonté Redoubt	1500m SW of Rose Cottage	8 E	626/2555	11
Bottom Wood	1500m SSE of Contalmaison church	8 E	6285/25571	12
Bow Trench	Just W of Serre Trench	7 W	623/2567	3
Bowery, The	450m SW of White City	7 W	6219/25658	5
Box Lane	1000m SE of Mouquet Farm	7 E	627/2561	7
Braemar Street	N of Chapes Spur	8 W	625/2557	9
Brandy Trench	NE off Ball Lane	8 E	626/2557	10
Brasserie Trench	240m E of Foncquevillers	7 W	621/2572	2
Braun Stellung	German 2nd Line	8 E	626+/2555+	8
Bray Street	SE of Ovillers Post	8 W	624/2558	8
Breslau Alley	NE off Mine Trench	8 E	630/2555	13
Breslau Salient	Just S of Breslau Trench	8 E	631/2555	14

Site / Trench	Location	Map	Map Ref.	Obj.
Breslau Trench	1.3km S of Montauban	8 E	630+/2555	14
Brick Lane	S from Alt Trench	8 E	631/2555	14
Bridgend	Just W of Hawthorne Mine	7 W	622/2565	5
Brigade HQ	Just E of Observation Wood	7 W	622/2567	3
Bright Alley	Runs S from Valley Trench	8 E	627/2556	12
Brimstone Trench	W of Ration Trench	7 E	626/2560	7
British Railway (1917)	Puisieux to Colincamps	7 W	619+/2567+	3
Broad Avenue	W of Gommecourt Park	7 W	621/2571	2
Broadway	W of Y Ravine	7 W	622/2564	5
Brock's Benefit	E of Mesnil	7 W	622/2562	7
Broomfield Street	E of Thiepval Wood	7 W	624/2562	7
Buchanan Avenue	E of Thiepval Wood	7 W	624/2561+	7
Buchanan Street	S of Y Ravine	7 W	622/2564	5
Bucket Trench	500m WSW of Pommiers Redoubt	8 E	629/2556	13
Bulgar Alley	Runs N 500m W of Mametz	8 E	629/2555	12
Bulgar Point	700m SSE of Mametz	8 E	629/2554	12
Bulgar Trench	W of Bulgar Point	8 E	629/2554	12
Bulgar Trench	Just N of Zollern Trench	7 W	625/2562	7
Bull's Eye	At NW Leipzig Salient	7 W	624/2561	7
Bund Support	700m SE of Pommiers Redoubt	8 E	630/2555	13
Bund Trench	700m SSE of Pommiers Redoubt	8 E	630/2555	13
Bunny Alley	Just S of Willow Stream & N of Mametz	8 E	629/2556	12
Bunny Wood	500m NNW of Mametz	8 E	628/2556	12
Burnwurk	520 m E of Jacob's Ladder	7 W	622/2565	5
Burrow Trench	Between Beaumont Hamel & Serre	7 W	623/2565+	5
Bury Avenue	Just E of Authuille village	7 W	624/2560	7
Caber Trench	E of Serre	7 W	623/2567	3
Cambridge Copse	1300m E of Carnoy	8 E	631/2554	14
Campbell Avenue	E of N Authuille	7 W	624/2560	7
Campbell Post	Near Leipzig Salient	7 W	624/2560	7
Campion Trench	Just SW of old Touvent Farm	7 W	622/2567	3
Cape Avenue	1200m NE of Foncquevillers	7 W	621/2572	2
Cardiff Street	500m W of Hawthorne Mine Crater	7 W	622/2565	5
Casement Trench	60m N of German's Wood	8 E	632/2555	14
Castle, The	800m SSE of Pommiers Redoubt	8 E	630/2555	13
Cat Street	E of Watling Street	7 W	622/2566	5
Cat Street Tunnel	Heidenkopf to Lager Alley	7 W	622/2566	5
Cateau Trench	E from Brigade H.Q.	7 W	622/2567	3
Caterpillar Trench	S from Caterpillar Wood	8 E	630/2557	13
Caterpillar Valley	Montauban sector	8 E	630/2557	14
Caterpillar Wood	1500m NW of Montauban church	8 E	630/2557	13
Caterpillar Wood/Copse	Just S of Thiepval Wood	7 W	624/2561	7
Causeway Side	Just N of Johnstone Post	7 W	624/2561+	7
Cemetery Trench	Just S of Mametz village	8 E	628/2555	12
Central Bluff	Thiepval sector	7 W	624+/2561+	7
Centre Way	1400m SE of Mouquet Farm	7 E	627/2561	7

Site / Trench	Location	Map	Map Ref.	Obj.
Chalk Pit	900m WNW of Fabrique Farm	7 W	620/25667	5
Chapes Spur	600m SSW of Lochnagar crater	8 W	625/2557	9
Charing Cross	S of Y Ravine	7 W	622/2564	5
Chasseur Hedge	Just N of new Touvent Farm	7 W	622/2568	3
Château Keep	N Maricourt	8 E	632/2554	14
Château Redoubt	S Thiepval	7 W	625/2561	7
Château Trench	Thiepval Wood	7 W	624/2561+	7
Chequer Bent St	Near Leipzig Redoubt	7 W	624/2561	7
Chorley Street	Authuille Wood	7 W	624/2559+	8
Chowbent Street	SW of Leipzig Salient	7 W	624/2561	7
Circus, The	E off Back Alley	8 E	629/2556	13
Clive Trench	Bet. Beaumont Hamel & Auchonvillers	7 W	621+/2564+	5
Clyde Avenue	E of Thiepval Wood	7 W	624/2561+	7
Cochrane Alley	880m SSW of Mametz	8 E	628/2554	12
Conniston Post	1300m N of Ovillers Post	8 W	624/2560	8
Conniston Street	from SE edge of Authuille Wood	8 W	624/2559	8
Constance Trench	WSW of Mouquet Farm	7 E	626+/2561+	7
Constitution Hill	S of Y Ravine	7 W	622/2564	5
Contalmaison	1800m S of Pozières	8 E	628/2558	10
Copper Trench	SE from Rose Alley	8 E	627/2555	12
Copse Trench	WSW of old Touvent Farm	7 W	622/2568	3
Coulee Trench	S of Pys	7 E	630/2565	7
Crater Lane	Joins Beaumont & Munich Trenches	7 W	622/2566	5
Crawl Boys Lane	1260m NNE of Foncquevillers	7 W	621/2573	2
Cripps Cut	Runs N from Pilk Street	7 W	622/2565	5
Cromerty Avenue	Thiepval Wood	7 W	624/2562	7
Cross Street	S of Gommecourt Park	7 W	621/2570	2
Crucifix Corner	700m ENE of Aveluy	7 W	623/2559	7
Crucifix Corner	Bet. Aveluy & Authuille	7 W	623/2559	7
Crucifix Trench	Just SW of Shelter Wood	8 E	627/2556	10
Crucifix, Mametz Civil cemetery	M/c gun opposed advance of 9th Devons	8E	285/25552	12
Crucifix, The	600m N of Thiepval	7 W	6254/25627	7
Crucifix, The	500m S of Birch Tree Wood	8 E	627/2557	10
Crucifix, The	Near W edge of Gommecourt Park	7 W	621/2571	2
Crucifix, The	500m W of Rossignol Wood	7 W	623/2570	2
Cuesclin Trench	NW of Staff Copse	7 W	621/2568	3
Danube Trench	500m SSW of Mametz Halt	8 E	628/2554+	12
Danube Trench – Thiepval	100m SSE of Thiepval	7 W	625/2560	7
Danzig Alley	Montauban road just out of Mametz	8 E	629/2555	12
Danzig Trench	Just SW of Cemetery Trench, Mametz	8 E	628/2555	12
Dart Lane	Just N of Lonely Lane	8 E	627/2556	11
Davnaar	Just E of Authuille Village	7 W	624/2560	7
Dell, The = Y Ravine	S of Beaumont Hamel	7 W	622+/25647	5
Derby Street	NW of Gommecourt Park	7 W	621/2571	2
Desiré Support	Contn. of Desiré Trench	7 E	627/2564	7

Site / Trench	Location	Map	Map Ref.	Obj.
Desiré Trench	N of Regina Trench W	7 E	627/2564	7
Dingle, The	130m E of Willow Patch	8 E	627/2557	11
Done's Redoubt	W Maricourt	8 E	632/2553	14
Donnet Post	400m N of Ovillers Post	8 W	624/2559	8
Donnet Street	S from Donnet Post	8 W	624/2558	8
Dorset Road	SW of Ovillers	8 W	624/2558	8
Dorset Street	800m SE of Ovillers Post	8 W	624/2558	8
Dressler Post	900m WSW of Y Sap crater	8 W	624/2557	9
Dublin Trench	500m N of German's Wood	8 E	632/2555	14
Dug-out	300m NW of Bailiff Wood	8 E	6275/25589	10
Dugout Trench	Just N of Warren Trench	8 E	631/2555	14
Duhollow Street	Glory Hole sector	8 W	625/2557	9
Dundee Street	Just N of Chapes Spur	8 W	625/2557	9
Dunfermline Street	SE of Ovillers Post	8 W	624/2558	8
Dunmow Trench	S from Brigade H.Q.	7 W	622/2567	3
Durham Street	Leipzig Salient	7 W	624/2561	7
Dyke Street	NW of Gommecourt Park	7 W	621/2571	2
E. Miraumont Rd	Runs S from Miraumont	7 E	628/2564+	5
East Trench	200m E of Caterpillar Trench	8 E	630/2557	13
Eczema Trench	E of Brigade H.Q.	7 W	622/2567	3
Eden Trench	SE of Gommecourt Park	7 W	622/2571	2
Eden Trench	W of Staff Copse	7 W	621/2568	3
Elbe Trench	SE of Gommecourt Park	7 W	622/2571	2
Elgin Avenue	Assy. pos. in Thiepval Wood. for ob6	7 W	624/2562	7
Ellis Square	Beaumont Hamel sector	7 W		5
Emden Trench	E off Austrian Junction	8 E	629/2556	13
Empress Trench	N of Konig Trench	8 E	626/2556	10
Engine Trench	Just W of Beaucourt/S/A	7 W	624/2564	5
Epte Trench	E of Gommecourt Park	7 W	622/2571	2
Erin Trench	Just S of The Maze	7 W	621/2571	2
Erstwaite Street	1600m NE of Ovillers Post	8 W	625/2559	8
Esau's Way	Contn. of Tenderloin Trench	7 W	622/2565	5
Essex Street	Continuation of Cardiff Street	7 W	622/2565	5
Essex Trench	Hawthorne Ridge	7 W	622/2565	5
Etch Trench	In Gommecourt Park	7 W	622/2571	2
Euston Dump	on Colincourt Road	7 W	620/2567	3
Exe Trench	Just S of The Maze	7 W	621+/2571	2
Fabeck Graben	see Fabeck Trench	7 E	627+/2561+	7
Fabeck Trench	Between Mouquet Farm and Courcelette	7 E	627+/2561+	7
Fable Trench	920m W of Rossignol Wood	7 W	623/2570	2
Face Trench	1850m SSE of The Maze	7 W	621/2571	2
Fact Trench	900m SE of Rossignol Wood	7 W	623/2570	2
Fair Trench	1730m SSE of The Maze	7 W	621/2571	2
Fall Trench	1120m W of Rossignol Wood	7 W	622/2570	2
Fame Trench	840m W of Rossignol Wood	7 W	623/2570	2
Fancy Trench	980m SW of Rossignol Wood	7 W	623/2570	2

Site / Trench	Location	Map	Map Ref.	Obj.
Farce Trench	Just E of Gommecourt Wood	7 W	622/2572	2
Farlock Trench	Runs SE from Ovillers	8 E	626/2559	8
Farm, la Grande	800m N of Thiepval	7 W	625/2563	7
Farmer Trench	920m SSE of The Maze	7 W	621/2571	2
Farmyard Trench	980m SSE of The Maze	7 W	621/2571	2
Fat Trench	980m SW of Rossignol Wood	7 W	623/2570	2
Fate Trench	1260m SSE of The Maze	7 W	621/2571	2
Favière Trench	400m S of German's Wood	8 E	632/2555	14
Feed Trench	640m SSE of The Maze	7 W	622/2571	2
Feint Trench	840m SSE of The Maze	7 W	622/2571	2
Fell Trench	E of Gommecourt Park	7 W	621/2571	2
Fellon Trench	E edge of Gommecourt Park	7 W	622/2571	2
Fellow Trench	E of Gommecourt Park	7 W	621/2571	2
Felt Trench	1060m SSE of The Maze	7 W	622/2571	2
Female Trench	500m SSE of The Maze	7 W	622/2571	2
Fen Trench	530m SSW of The Maze	7 W	621/2571	2
Fern Trench	640m SSE of the Maze	7 W	622/2571	2
Ferret Trench	560m S of The Maze	7 W	621/2571	2
Feste Soden	SSE of Serre	7 W	624/2567	3
Fethard Street	W of Y Ravine	7 W	622/2564	5
Fetlock Trench	Runs SE from 1200m E of La Boisselle	8 E	627/2557+	10
Fettor Trench	1120m SSE of The Maze	7 W	621/2571	2
Feud Trench	E of Gommecourt Park	7 W	621/2571	2
Fever Trench	890m SSE of the Maze	7 W	622/2570	2
Field Trench	560m W of The Maze	7 W	621/2571	2
Fifth Avenue	W of Gommecourt Park	7 W	621/2571	2
Fig Trench	800m SW of The Maze	7 W	621/2571	2
Fight Trench	In Gommecourt Park	7 W	621/2571	2
Fillet Trench	In Gommecourt Park	7 W	621/2571	2
Film Trench	Just E of The Maze	7 W	622/2571	2
Fin Trench	470m WSW of The Maze	7 W	621/2571	2
Find Trench	890m WSW of The Maze	7 W	621/2571	2
Fine Trench	In Gommecourt Park	7 W	621/2571	2
Firm Trench	550m SW of The Maze	7 W	621/2571	2
Fish Trench	600m SW of The Maze	7 W	621/2571	2
Fist Trench	In Gommecourt Park	7 W	621/2571	2
Fix Trench	550m W of The Maze	7 W	621/2571	2
Flag Ave Trench	SW from Matthew Copse	7 W	622/2567	3
Flank Trench	Runs E from just N of Serre	7 W	624/2567	5
Fob Trench	1960m WNW of Rettemoy Farm	7 W	622/2572	2
Focus Trench	550m WNW of The Maze	7 W	621/2571	2
Foe Trench	50m W of Gommecourt Wood	7 W	621/2571	2
Folk Trench	Just W of Gommecourt Wood	7 W	622/2572	2
Folly Trench	W of Gommecourt Wood	7 W	622/2572	2
Font Trench	Just E of Gommecourt Wood	7 W	622/2572	2
Font Trench	W of Gommecourt Wood	7 W	621/2571	2
Food Trench	W of Gommecourt Wood	7 W	622/2572	2

Site / Trench	Location	Map	Map Ref.	Obj.
Fool Trench	W of Gommecourt Wood	7 W	622/2572	2
Foolery Trench	140m W of Gommecourt Wood	7 W	621/2571	2
Foot Trench	890m W of Pigeon Wood	7 W	622/2572	2
Forage Trench	E of Gommecourt Wood	7 W	622/2572	2
Ford Trench	40m W of Gommecourt Wood	7 W	621/2571	2
Forehead Trench	Just E of Gommecourt Wood	7 W	622/2572	2
Foreign Trench	Just E of Gommecourt Wood	7 W	622/2572	2
Foresight Trench	Runs NE from top of Gommecourt Wood	7 W	621/2571	2
Fork Trench	Runs NW from Gommecourt Wood	7 W	621/2571	2
Form Trench	Just E of Gommecourt Wood	7 W	622/2572	2
Forres Avenue	Thiepval Wood	7 W	624/2561+	7
Fort Grosvenor	1920m WNW of Sheffield Park	7 W	621/2568	3
Fort Hindenburg	Bet. Leipzip Sal. & Wonderwork	7 W	624/2561	7
Fort Jackson	Newfoundland Park	7 W	622/2564	5
Fort Lemberg	N of Fort Hindenburg	7 W	623/2560	7
Fort Moulin	1800m SWS of Y Ravine	7 W	621/2563	5
Fort Prowse	2200m SW of Y Ravine	7 W	621/2563	5
Fort Southdown	1600m W of old Touvent Farm	7 W	621/2568	3
Fort Trench	Just E of Gommecourt Wood	7 W	622/2572	2
Fortune Trench	W of Pigeon Wood	7 W	623/2572	2
Fount Trench	170m W of Gommecourt Wood	7 W	621/2571	2
Fowl Trench	700m W of Pigeon Wood	7 W	622/2572	2
Fox Trench	640m W of Pigeon Wood	7 W	622/2572	2
Foxbar Street	E of Johnstone Post	7 W	624/2561	7
Frankfort Trench	NE of Beaumont Hamel	7 W	623/2565+	5
French Street	S of Johnstone Post	7 W	624/2561+	7
Fricourt Farm	840m NNE of Fricourt	8 E	6275/25568	10
Fricourt Spur	High ground to W of Fricourt	8 E	626/2556	11
Fricourt Trench	SSE from Tambour Mines	8 E	626+/2555	11
Fritz Avenue	800m N of Serre	7 W	624/2568	3
Fritz Trench	1800m E of Fricourt Farm	8 E	629/2556	12
Frontier Lane	N from Beaumont Hamel	7 W	622/2566	5
Fuel Trench	1570m NNE of Gommecourt Park	7 W	623/2573	2
Fume Trench	NE of Gommecourt Wood	7 W	622/2572	2
Fun Trench	1120m NE of Gommecourt Park	7 W	623/2572	2
Fungus Trench	500m NNE of Pigeon Wood	7 W	623/2573	2
Funk Trench	1820m NNE of Gommecourt Park	7 W	623/2573	2
Fur Trench	1600m NNE of Gommecourt Park	7 W	623/2573	2
Furness Street	Just W of Ovillers	8 W	625/2559	8
Furrier Trench	1450m NNE of Gommecourt Park	7 W	623/2573	2
Fury Trench	1400m NNE of Gommecourt Park	7 W	622/2573	2
Fuse Trench	NE of Gommecourt Wood	7 W	622/2572	2
Fuss Trench	1820m NNE of Gommecourt Park	7 W	623/2573	2
Galgen	see Keats Redan	8 W	625/2558	8
Gemmel Trench	E of Thiepval Wood	7 W	624/2561+	7
George Street	Thiepval Wood	7 W	624/2561+	7
German Tambour	Just S of Triple Tambour Mines	8 E	626/2555	11

Site / Trench	Location	Map	Map Ref.	Obj.
German's Wood (Schrapnell Way)	1600m SSE of Montauban	8 E	632/2555	14
Giants Causeway	Between River Ancre & Beaucourt	7 W	624/2564	5
Gin Alley	800m S of Scotts Redoubt	8 E	627/2556	10
Glatz Alley	from Glatz Redoubt to Favière Trench	8 E	632/2555+	14
Glatz Redoubt	800m SSE of Montauban	8 E	632/2556	14
Glory Hole, The	1000m SW of La Boisselle church	8 W	625/2557	9
Glory Lane	Continuation of Munich Trench	7 W	623/2566	5
Goat Redoubt	Between Mouquet Fm. & Stuff Redoubt	7 W	626/2561+	7
Gommecourt Park	SW of Foncquevillers	7 W	621/2571	2
Gommecourt village	1300m SE Foncquevillers	7 W	622/2571	2
Gommecourt Wood (Bois du Sartel)	SW of Foncquevillers	7 W	622/2571+	2
Gooch Street	W of Gommecourt Park	7 W	621/2571	2
Gordon Castle	Thiepval Wood	7 W	624/2562	7
Gordon Dump	E of La Boiselle	8 E	626/2558	9
Gordon Post	700m NE of Lochnagar crater	8 E	626/2558	10
Gordon Trench	Serre sector	7 W	622/2568	3
Gouroch Street	E of Thiepval Wood	7 W	624/2561+	7
Govan Street	E of Thiepval Wood	7 W	624/2561+	7
Gowrie Street	Adjacent to La Bois. civil cem.	8 W	625/2558	9
Granatloch	Leipzig Salient	7 W	624/2561	7
Grandcourt Trench	E from S Grandcourt	7 E	627/2564	7
Great Northern Railway	La Signy to Touvent Farm	7 W	621+/2567+	3
Greenock Avenue	Just NE of Authuille village	7 W	624/2560	7
Halt, The	Mametz old Railway Station	8 E	628/2555	12
Hamel Bridge	Bridge over Ancre ESE of Hamel	7 W	623/2562	7
Hamilton Avenue	E of Thiepval Wood	7 W	624/2561+	7
Hammerhead Sap	E of Thiepval Wood	7 W	624/2561+	7
Hansa Line	N of Schwaben Rdbt. to R. Ancre	7 W	625/2563+	5
Happy Valley	Continuation of Pilk Street	7 W	622/2565	5
Hare Lane	E of Triple Tambour Mines	8 E	626/2556	10
Hawthorne Ridge Redoubt Mine	500m W of Beaumont Hamel	7 W	622/2565	5
Hawthorne Road	W of Beaumont Hamel	7 W	622/2565	5
Haymarket	W of Y Ravine	7 W	622/2564	5
Heaton Road	S of old Beaumont Road	7 W	622/2565	5
Heiden Kopf	Site of Serre Rd. No. 2 Cem.	7 W	622/2566	3
Heligoland	700m E of Lochnagar crater	8 E	626/2558	10
Hennslow Road	S of old Beaumont Road	7 W	622/2565	5
Hessian Trench	Just north of Zollern Redoubt	7 E	626/25635	7
Hidden Lake	Mametz sector	8 E	627/2554+	12
Hidden Lane	SSW from Hidden Wood	8 E	628/2554	12
Hidden Wood	1100m SE Fricourt church	8 E	628/25552	12
High Trench	Runs E from N Mouquet Farm	7 E	627/2561	7
Hindenburg Trench	Just N of Leipzig Salient	240	624/2561	7
Hodder Street	N of Ovillers Post	8 W	624/2558	9
Hohenzollern Trench	Near Wonder Werk	7 W	624+/2561+	7

Site / Trench	Location	Map	Map Ref.	Obj.
Hope Trench	Just N of Y Ravine	7 W	622/2564	5
Horseshoe Trench	NE of Scots Redoubt	8 E	626/2557+	9
Horwich Street	W of Conniston Post	8 W	624/2560	8
Hospital Trench	300m ESE of Hawthorne Crater	7 W	622/2565	5
Houghton Street	300m E of Ovillers Post	8 W	624/2558	8
Hunters Trench	S of Hawthorne Mine	7 W	622/2564	5
Hyde Park Corner	S of Y Ravine	7 W	622/2564	5
Iban Trench	400m ENE of Rettemoy Farm	7 W	624/2572	2
Ilot, The	Group of T's la Bois. civ. cem.	8 W	625/2558	9
Inch Street	Adjacent to Glory Hole	8 W	625/2558	9
Indre Trench	550m W of Rettemoy Farm	7 W	623/2572	2
Indus Trench	W of Bois du Biez	7 W	622/2571	2
Inverness Avenue	Thiepval Wood	7 W	624/2562	7
Inverrary Street	Just W of Leipzig Salient	7 W	624/2561	7
Iona Street	Just W of Leipzig Salient	7 W	624/2561	7
Islay Street	Just W of Leipzig Salient	7 W	624/2561	7
Itchin Trench	670m SW of Rettemoy Farm	7 W	623/2571	2
Jacob's Ladder	450m NW of Hawthorne Crater	7 W	622/2565	5
Jäger-Höhe	1700m E of La Boisselle	8 E	627/2558	9
Jam Street	700m NW of Serre	7 W	623/2568	3
Jean Bart Trench	Nr. new Touvent Farm	7 W	622/2568	3
Jenburg Street	Just N of Leipzig Salient	7 W	624/2561	7
John Copse	Assy point for Serre attack	7 W	623/2568	5
John O'Gaunt St	Just W of Ovillers	8 W	625/2559	8
Johnstone Post	SE corner of Thiepval Wood	7 W	624/2562	7
Joseph Trench	ESE of Thiepval	7 W	6255/25615	7
Jura Street	Just W of Leipzig Salient	7 W	624/3561	7
Kaiser Lane	540m N of Serre	7 W	624/2569	3
Kaiser Str.	700m E of La Boisselle	8 E	626/2558	10
Kaiser's Oak Tree	SW corner of Gommecourt Wood	7 W	6214/25712	5
Kasino Point Mine	1000m N of Carnoy	8 E	6302/25552	14
Kaufmann Gr.	400m NE of Lochnagar crater	8 E	626/2558	10
Keats Redan	1000m NW of Lochnagar crater	8 W	625/2558	9
Keep, The	Just S of Gommecourt Park	7 W	621/2571	2
Keep, The	Authuille village	7 W	624/2560	7
Kendri Trench	1000m NW of Courcelette	7 E	628/2563	7
Kern Redoubt	E edge of Gommecourt Park	7 W	622/2571	2
Kerrera Street	Just W of Leipzig Salient	7 W	624/2561	7
Kiel Lane	300m SW of Mametz Halt	8 E	628/2555	12
Kilberry	Just E of Authuille village	7 W	624/2560	7
Kilmun Street	Just W of Leipzig Salient	7 W	624/2561	7
Kilometer Lane	NE from Auchonvillers/Serre Rd.	7 W	621/2566	5
King Street	Runs E fr. Tenderloin Trench	7 W	622/2565	5
Kingsgate Street	Just N of Chapes Spur	8 W	625/2557	9
Kintyre Trench	E of Authuille village	7 W	624/2560	7
Kipper Trench	600m SE of Scots Redoubt	8 E	626/2557	9
Kirkaldy Street	800m ESE of Ovillers Post	8 W	625/2558	8
Kitchen Trench	SSE off Rose Alley	8 E	627/2555	12

Site / Trench	Location	Map	Map Ref.	Obj.
Kite Copse	E of Pigeon Wood	7 W	623/2572	2
König Lane	Just N of Fricourt	8 E	627/2556	11
König Trench	N-S through Triple Tambour Mines	8 E	626/2555	11
La Boisselle village	1200m SSW Ovillers	8 W	625/2558	9
La Brayelle Farm	N of Pigeon Wood	7 W	623/2572	2
Lager Alley	E of Munich Trench towards Serre	7 W	623+/2566+	5
Lancashire Lane (Zollern Graben)	ENE from Thiepval towards Goat Redoubt	7 W	625/2562	7
Lancaster Avenue	600N of Ovillers Post	8 W	624/2559	8
Lanwick/Lerwick Trench	N from Jacob's Ladder	7 W	622/2565	5
Lattorf Graben	E of D929 NE of La Boiselle	8 E	627/2559	9
Leave Avenue	Just N of Beaumont Alley	7 W	623/2565	5
Legend Trench	Between Beaumont Hamel & Serre	7 W	623/2565+	5
Lehmgruben Hohe	1000m ESE of Lochnagar crater	8 E	626/2557	9
Lehmgrubenhohe	NW of Fricourt	8 E	626/2556	9
Leicester Street	NW of Gommecourt Park	7 W	621/2571	2
Leipzig Salient	1200m SSW of Thiepval	7 W	62475/2561	7
Lemberg Trench	Just N of Leipzig Salaient	7 W	624/2561	7
Limerick Junction	W of Y Ravine	7 W	622/2564	5
Lincoln Lane	NW of Gommecourt Park	7 W	621/2571	2
Lincoln Redoubt	500m N of Scots Redoubt	8 E	626/2557	9
Little Z	810m WNW of Pigeon Wood	7 W	622/2572	2
Loch Aire Street	Just W of Leipzig Salient	7 W	624/2561	7
Lochnagar Mine	500m SSE of La Boiselle	8 E	625/2557	9
Lochnagar Street	Just N of Chapes Spur	8 W	625/2557	9
Lonely Copse	400m N of Fricourt	8E	6273/25564	11
Lonely Lane	400m N of Red Cottage	8 E	626/2556	11
Lonely Trench	Just N of Fricourt village	8 E	627/2556	11
Loop Trench	N from E end of The Loop	8 E	630/2556	13
Loop, The	600m SE of Pommiers Redoubt	8 E	630/2555	13
Lorna Pass	Just W of Leipzig Salient	7 W	624/2561	7
Lozenge Alley	Runs W of Fricourt Farm	8 E	627/2556	11
Lozenge Trench	980m S of Scotts Redoubt	8 E	627/2556	11
Lozenge, The	see 1406 Wundt Werk	7 W	625/2567	3
Lucky Way	Due S of Grandcourt	7 E	626/2564	5
Luke Copse	Assy point for Serre attack	7 W	623/2568	3
Lunar Trench	Runs NW from the Bowery	7 W	621/2565	5
Machine Gun Wood	600m NW of Château Keep	8 E	631/2554	14
Madam Trench	E corner of Rossignol Wood	7 W	624/2570	2
Maid Trench	Just SE of Rossignol Wood	7 W	624/2570	2
Main Trench	SW of Rossignol Wood	7 W	624/2570	2
Maison grise sap	E of Thiepval Wood	7 W	624/2561+	7
Male Trench	NE of Rossignol Wood	7 W	624/2570	2
Mama Trench	450m SE of Rossignol Wood	7 W	624/2570	2
Mametz Trench	W of Bulgar Trench	8 E	628/2555	12
Mametz village	1600m E Fricourt	8 E	628/2555	12
Man Trench	NE edge of Rossignol Wood	7 W	624/2570	2
Manchester Alley	N & S from Silesia Trench	8 E	631/2555	14

Site / Trench	Location	Map	Map Ref.	Obj.
Mansel Copse	1000m S of Mametz	8 E	6286/25549	12
Mansel Copse, German Line	Mansel Copse	8 E	62834/2555	12
Map Trench	Just SW of Rossignol Wood	7 W	623/2570	2
Maple Trench	380m E of Pommiers Redoubt	8 E	629/2556	13
Mark Copse	Assy point for attack on Serre	7 W	623/2568	3
Market Cross	Just Sw of Dressler Post	8 W	624/2557	9
Market Trench	740m N of Thiepval	7 W	624+/2561+	7
Marlborough Wood	1400m NW of Montauban church	8 E	6309/25578	14
Marsh Trench	Just S of Rossignol Wood	7 W	624/2570	2
Martin's Trench	N from Thiepval to Schwaben Redoubt	7 W	625/2562	7
Mary Redan	500m SSE from S tip of Y Ravine	7 W	622/2564	5
Mary Redan Trench	S of Beaumont Hamel	7 W	622/2564	5
Mash Valley	5/600m W of La Boisselle	8 W	625/2558	9
Mat Trench	Just SW of Rossignol Wood	7 W	623/2570	2
Match Trench	750m SE of Rossignol Wood	7 W	624/2570	2
Matthew Copse	Assy point for attack on Serre	7 W	623/2567	3
Meadow Trench	360m NNW of Rossignol Wood	7 W	623/2571	2
Meed Trench	300m NW of Rossignol Wood	7 W	623/2571	2
Meet Trench	Just NW of Rossignol Wood	7 W	623/2570	2
Mend Trench	420m N of Rossignol Wood	7 W	623/2571	2
Mere Trench	750m NW of Rossignol Wood	7 W	623/2571	2
Mersey Street	Near Leipzig Redoubt	7 W	624+/2561+	7
Mersey Trench	Thiepval sector	7 W	624+/2561+	7
Mess Trench	980m NW of Rossignol Wood	7 W	623/2571	2
Metal Trench	Just E of Bois du Biez	7 W	624/2571	2
Middle Avenue	Runs N off Back Trench	8 E	631/2555	13
Middle Trench	Behind Foncquevillers	7 W	621/2573	2
Midland Trench	NW of Gommecourt Park	7 W	621/2571	2
Midway Line	Schwaben Rdt to Mouquet Farm	7 W	626/2561	7
Might Trench	550m WNW of Bois du Biez	7 W	623/2571	2
Mill Bridge	Bridge over Ancre near mill Authuille	7 W	623/2560	7
Mill Road	SE from N of Hamel	7 W	624/2563	7
Mill Trench	Just N of St. Pierre Divion	7 W	624/2563	5
Mill Trench	Just SW of Montauban	8 E	631/2556	14
Mill, Beaumont Hamel	E of Beaumont Hamel station	7 W	624/2564	5
Mill, The	N Authuille	7 W	623/2560	7
Mince Trench	550m E of Bois du Biez	7 W	623/2571	2
Mine Alley	Just S of Montauban	8 E	631/2556	14
Mine Trench	E from Casino Point Mine	8 E	630/2555	13
Mining tunnel entry (one of)	La Boisselle civil cemetery	8 W	625/2558	9
Mint Trench	280m NNE of Rettemoy Farm	7 W	624/2572	2
Minx Trench	330m S of Pigeon Wood	7 W	623/2572	2
Mist Trench	Just N of E edge of Bois du Biez	7 W	624/2571	2
Mole Trench	420m ENE of Pigeon Wood	7 W	623/2572	2
Monk Trench	420m NW of Rettemoy Farm	7 W	624/2572	2
Monk Trench	Just S of Staff Copse	7 W	622/2567	3

Site / Trench	Location	Map	Map Ref.	Obj.
Monkey Trench	430m NW of Rettemoy Farm	7 W	624/2572	2
Montauban Alley	Caterpillar Wd to N of Bernafay Wood	8 E	631+/2557	13
Montauban village	3100m ENE Mametz	8 E	631/2556	14
Moon Trench	470m NNE of Rettemoy Farm	7 W	624/2572	2
Mop Trench	Just E of Pigeon Wood	7 W	623/2572	2
Moss Trench	640m E of Pigeon Wood	7 W	623/2572	2
Mound Keep	NE Maricourt	8 E	632/2554	14
Mound Keep	Just N of Authuille Wood	7 W	623/2561	7
Mound, The	N of Stuff Redoubt, Thiepval sector	7 W	625/2563	7
Mound, The	550m W of St. Pierre Divion	7 W	624/2563	5
Mound, The	250m E of Bulgar Point	8 E	629/2554	12
Mouquet Farm	1600m NW of Pozières	7 E	627/25617	7
Mouquet Farm Track	Park Lane to Mouquet Farm	7 E	627/2561	7
Mouquet Quarry	200m S of Mouquet Farm	7 E	6269/25615	7
Mouquet Switch	from Mouquet Farm towards Schwaben Rdbt	7 E	626/2562	7
Mouse Trench	550m E of Pigeon Wood	7 W	623/2572	2
Muck Trench	E of Munich New Trench & Triangle	7 W	624/2565	5
Mud Trench	Just N of Pigeon Wood	7 W	623/2572	2
Mug Trench	615m E of la Brayelle Farm	7 W	623/2572	2
Munich Trench	Between Serre & Beaumont Hamel	7 W	623/2565+	5
Music Trench	Just N of Pigeon Wood	7 W	623/2572	2
Mute Trench	300m E of la Brayelle Farm	7 W	623/2572	2
Muzzle Trench	550m E of la Brayelle Farm	7 W	623/2572	2
Nab Valley	NE through Authuille Wood	8 W	625/2560	7
Nab Valley (later Blightly Valley)	E of Leipzig Salient	7 W	624/2561	7
Nab Wood	1600m NE of Aveluy XR	8 W	624/2559	7
Nab, The	550m SE of Leipzig Redoubt	7 W	625/2560	7
Nairne Trench	N of Serre	7 W	624/2568	3
Nameless Farm (Bock Farm)	400m SE of Gommecourt Park	7 W	622/2570	2
Napier's Redoubt	SW Maricourt	8 E	632/2553	14
Naze, The	Just W of Leipzig Salient	7 W	624/2560	7
Neilstone Street	E of Thiepval Wood	7 W	624/2561+	7
Nestler Hohlen	ENE of Fricourt Farm	8 E	627/2556	11
New Beaumont Rd	Achonvillers to Beaumont Hamel	7 W	621+/2565	5
New Munich Trench	300m E of Munich Trench	7 W	6235/25655	5
New Street	W of Gommecourt Park	7 W	621/2571	2
Nord Alley	Montauban to Glatz Redoubt	8 E	631/2556	14
Nord Werk	900m NNE of Ovillers	8 E	626/2560	7
North Causeway	Just SW of Thiepval Wood	7 W	623/2561	7
North Street	Just S of Watling Street	7 W	622/2566	5
Northern Avenue	NW from Red Cottage	7 W	621/2567	3
Nose, The	300m SSE of Lochnagar crater	8 E	626/2557	9

Site / Trench	Location	Map	Map Ref.	Obj.
Nottingham Street	NW of Gommecourt Park	7 W	621/2571	2
Oakham Trench	W of Gommecourt Wood	7 W	621/2571	2
Oban Avenue	Just E of Authuille village	7 W	624/2560	7
Oblong Wood	Bet. Thiepval and Thiepval Wood	7 W	624/2561+	7
Odiham Trench	Just W of Gommecourt Park	7 W	622/2572	2
Ohio Trench	Just N of Gommecourt Wood	7 W	622/2572	2
Old Beaumont Rd	S of new Beaumont Road	7 W	621/2565	5
Old Mill	Miraumont	7 E	627/2565	5
Orange Trench	550m W of Pigeon Wood	7 W	622/2572	2
Orchard Alley	800m W of the Halt, Mametz old station	8 E	627/2555	12
Orchard Copse	Just N of The Twins	8 E	630/2556	14
Orchard Trench	300m W of Mametz	8 E	628/2555	12
Orchard, The	Junction of Orchard & Willow Trenches	8 E	628/2555	12
Orionoco Trench	Just N of Gommecourt Wood	7 W	622/2572	2
Orleans Trench	Just W of Gommecourt Wood	7 W	622/2572	2
Oundle Trench	Just W of Gommecourt Wood	7 W	622/2572	2
Ouse Trench	ENE of Gommecourt Wood	7 W	622/2572	2
Ovillers Post	1100m WNW of Y Sap crater	8 W	624/2558	8
Ovillers Spur	N of Ovillers	8 E	625/2559	8
Ovillers Tramway	La Boisselle to Ulverston	8 W	625/2558+	8
Ovillers village	1200m NNE La Boisselle	8 E	626/2559	8
Oxford Copse	1200m ESE of Carnoy	8 E	631/2554	14
Oxus Trench	NE of Gommecourt Park	7 W	623/2572	2
Padré Street	E of Ovillers Post	8 W	624/2558	8
Paisley Avenue	Thiepval sector	7 W	624+/2561+	7
Paisley Dump	Thiepval sector	7 W	624+/2561	7
Palestine Trench	Communication Trench Serre	7 W	623/2567	3
Papen Trench	800m WNW of Mametz Halt	8 E	627/2555	12
Parallelogram	see Schwaben Redoubt	7 W	625/2562	7
Park Corner	680m SSW of Y Ravine	7 W	622/2563	5
Passerelle de Magenta	Just SW of Thiepval Wood	7 W	623/2561	7
Patch Alley	650m S of Scots Redoubt	8 E	627/2557	10
Peake Woods	800m SW of Contalmaison church	8 E	6277/2558	10
Pear Trench	Just W of Apple Alley	8 E	627/2555	12
Pendant Alley West	400m ESE of Serre	7 W	624/2567	3
Pendant Copse	940m SE Serre centre	7 W	6247/25671	5
Pendant Trench	N of Pendant Copse	7 W	624/2567	3
Pendlehill Street	1300m NE of Ovillers Post	8 W	625/2559	8
Piccadilly	S of Y Ravine	7 W	622/2564	5
Pigeon Wood	1600m NE of Gommecourt	7 W	623/2572	2
Pilk Street	S of old Beaumont Road	7 W	622/2565	5
Pill Trench	NW of Gommecourt Park	7 W	621/2571	2
Pip Street	1500m S of Thiepval	7 W	625/2561	7
Pitlochry Street	NNW of Chapes Spur	8 W	625/2557	9
Point 110	S of Fricourt on 110m contour line	8 E	627/2554	11

Site / Trench	Location	Map	Map Ref.	Obj.
Point 60	240m E of S tip of Y Ravine	7 W	622/2564	5
Point 66	Strong point in Desirée Trench	7 E	627/2563	5
Point 71 N	1400m S of Tambour Mines	8 E	626/2554	11
Point 89	80m of W end of Y Ravine	7 W	622/2564	5
Pole Trench	1000m SE of Mouquet Farm	7 E	626/2560	7
Pommiers Lane	Runs SE from Pommiers Redoubt	8 E	630/2556	13
Pommiers Redoubt	E of Danzig Alley	8 E	630/2556	13
Pommiers Trench	S of Pommiers Redoubt	8 E	630/2555	13
Poodles, The	Just N of Fricourt Farm	8 E	627/2556	12
Pope's Nose	1200m NNW of Thiepval	7 W	6244/2562	7
Popoff Lane	1400m N of Carnoy	8 E	630/2555	13
Port Louis	300m SW of Ovillers Post	8 W	624/2558	8
Prince Street	NNE from Leipzig Salient	7 W	624/2561	7
Prindlehill Street	Just W of Ovillers	8 W	625/2559	8
Puisieux Trench	Runs S from E end of Flank Trench	7 W	624/2567	5
Purfleet	Just W of König Lane	8 E	626/2555	11
Pys village	NW of Le Sars	7 E	629/2565	5
Quadrilateral – Gommecourt	835m E of Kern Redoubt	7 W	622/2571	2
Quadrilateral (B.Ham/ Serre)	80m S of Serre Brit. Cem. No. 2	7 W	622/2566	5
Quadrilateral (Heindenkopf)	80m S of Serre Brit. Cem. No. 2	7 W	622/2566	3
Quadrilateral, Thiepval	Thiepval sector	7 W	624+/2561+	7
Quarry Trench	W to E from S of Mouquet Fm	7 E	626+/2561	7
Queen's Cross St	E of Thiepval Wood	7 W	624/2561+	7
Queen's Redoubt	1000m W of Triple Tambour Mines	8 W	625/2556	10
Quergraben II	E of D929 NE of La Boisselle	8 E	627/2559	9
Quergraben III	ENE of Pozières	8 E	626/2558	9
Rabbit Lane	E of Triple Tambour Mines N	8 E	626/2555	10
Radcliffe Street	Just E of Authuille village	7 W	624/2560	7
Railland Trench	Just E of Authuille village	7 W	624/2560	7
Railway Avenue Trench	Nr. Euston Dump	7 W	620/2567	3
Railway Road	On the Beaucourt-Miraumont road	7 E	626/2565	5
Railway Trench	700m NNW of Beaucourt	7 W	623/2564	5
Railway Valley	Montauban sector	8 E	631/2555+	14
Ration Trench (Gierich Weg)	NW of Pozières	7 E	627/2560	7
Raymond Avenue	NW of Gommecourt Park	7 W	621/2571	2
Red Cottage	N Fricourt	8 E	627/2556	11
Red Cottage	NNW of Basin Wood	7 W	621/2567	3
Red Lane	W of Fricourt N	8 E	627/2556	11
Red Trench	1200m SSE of Mouquet Farm	7 E	627/2561	7
Red Trench	S from Red La to Rabbit Lane	8 E	626/2555	12
Redan Ridge	N of Beaumont Hamel	7 W	622/2566	5
Redan Ridge Redoubt	400m N of Bergwerk	7 W	622/2566	5

Site / Trench	Location	Map	Map Ref.	Obj.
Redoubt Alley	W of Beaucourt	7 W	624/2565	5
Regent Street	S of Y Ravine	7 W	622/2564	5
Regent Street	NW of Gommecourt Park	7 W	621/2571	2
Regina Trench	Runs from N Thiepval			
- West	to Grandcourt	7 W	625+/2562	7
Rettemoy Farm	2300m ENE Gommecourt	7 W	624/2572	2
Ribble Street	Near Ovillers Post	8 E	626/2559	7
Ribble Street	S from Donnet Post	8 W	624/2558	8
Ridge Redoubt	SW of Serre	7 W	623/2567	3
River Trench	Just E of Puisieux Trench	7 W	624/2567	5
Rivington Street	1300m NE of Ovillers Post	8 W	625/2559	8
Road Trench	from Leipzig Salient towards memorial	7 W	624/2561	7
Rob Roy Trench	E & W of Railway Hollow	7 W	622/2568	3
Roberts Avenue	NW of Gommecourt Park	7 W	621/2571	2
Roberts Trench	Near Beaucourt	7 W	624+/2564+	5
Rolland Trench	N from Great Northern Trench	7 W	622/2567	3
Roman Road Trench	Commun. Trench Sucrerie	7 W	620/2566	3
Rooney's Sap	300m SW of Hawthorne Crater	7 W	622/2565	5
Rose Alley	SE Fricourt	8 E	627/2555	12
Rose Cottage	Fricourt E	8 E	627/2555	12
Rose Trench	550m NW of Mametz Halt	8 E	628/2555	12
Ross Castle	Thiepval Wood	7 W	624/2561+	7
Ross Street	Thiepval Wood	7 W	624/2561+	7
Rossignol Farm	Near Rossignol Wood	7 W	624/2570	5
Rossignol Wood	SW of Bois de Biez	7 W	623/2570	2
Rothes Street	Thiepval Wood	7 W	624/2562	7
Rotten Row	NW of Gommecourt Park	7 W	621/2571	2
Rough Trench	60m E of Seaforth Trench	7 W	622/2565	5
Round Wood	300m SE of Scots Redoubt	8 E	6271/25572	10
Round Wood Alley	S edge of Scots Redoubt	8 E	627/2556	9
Rump Trench	N of Beaumont Hamel	7 W	623/2565	5
Rycroft Street	1000m NE of Ovillers Post	8 W	625/2559	8
Sackville Street	Just N of Redan Ridge	7 W	622/2567	3
Sandra Street	Just W of Leipzig Salient	7 W	624/2561	7
Sauchiehall Street	E of Thiepval Wood	7 W	624/2561+	7
Sausage Redoubt	600m E of Lochnagar crater	8 E	626/2557	9
Sausage Valley	1000m S of La Boisselle	8 W	625/2557	9
Schrapnell Way	see German's Wood	8 E	632/2555	14
Schwaben Höhe	200m N of Lochnagar crater	8 E	626/2557	9
Schwaben Nest	Just N of Gommecourt Wood	7 W	622/2572	2
Schwaben Redoubt	900m NNE of XR at Thiepval	7 W	624+/2562+	7
Schwaben Trench, Thiepval	Mouquet Farm to Thiepval	7 W	6258/2562	7
Scots Redoubt	400m W of Birch Tree Wood	8 E	627/2556	9
Seaforth Trench	Runs S from Happy Valley	7 W	622/2565	5
Serheb Road	NW out of Serre	7 W	623/2568	3
Serre Trench	Just W of Serre	7 W	623/2567+	3
Serre village	2000m SW Puisieux	7 W	624/2567	3

Site / Trench	Location	Map	Map Ref.	Obj.
Shaftesbury Ave	S of Y Ravine	7 W	622/2564	5
Shelter Wood	1500m SSW of Contalmaison	8 E	627/2557	10
Shrapnel Trench	Ovillers	8 W	625/2559+	8
Shrine Alley	Mametz to Mametz civil cemetery	8 E	628/2555	12
Shrine, The	German m/c gun post in Mametz Civ. Cem.	8 E	62855/25554	12
Sickle Trench	N of Ovillers	8 E	626/2560	8
Sigel Graben	1300m ESE of Lochnagar crater	8 E	627/2557	9
Silesia Alley	N & S from Silesia Trench	8 E	631/2555	14
Silesia Trench	1200m S of Montauban	8 E	631/2555	14
Sinclair Road	Authuille village	7 W	624/2560	7
Sixth Street	W of Gommecourt Park	7 W	621/2571	2
Skyline Trench	SSW of Mouquet Farm	7 E	626/2561	7
Slight Valley	900m E of Ovillers	8 E	6267/25593	8
Soda Trench	600m SSW of Scots Redoubt	8 E	626/2557	10
South Bluff	Thiepval sector	7 W	624+/2561+	7
South Causeway	Just SW of Thiepval Wood	7 W	623/2561	7
South Sausage	N of Empress Trench	8 E	627/2557	10
South Trench	S of Montauban	8 E	631/2556	14
Southern Avenue	S of Brigade H.Q.	7 W	622/2567	3
Southern Trench	Just S of Montauban	8 E	631/2556	14
Square Wood	Just SW of Bois de Biez	7 W	624/2571	2
St. Andrew's Ave	Comm. Trench west from Usna Hill	8 W	624/2558	9
St. Helen's	S from Tenderloin Street	7 W	622/2565	5
St. James's Street	S of Y Ravine	7 W	622/2564	5
St. John's Road	Auchonvillers towards Hamel	7 W	621+/2564	5
St. John's Road Trench	Assy point for attack on Y Ravine	7 W	622+/2564	5
St. Martin's Lane	W of Gommecourt Park	7 W	621/2571	2
St. Pierre Divion	1600m NNW Thiepval	7 W	624/2563	5
St. Vincent Street	Just W of Ovillers	8 W	625/2559	8
Stabgraben	200m E of D929 NE of La Boisselle	8 E	627/2559	9
Staff Copse	Site of old Touvent Farm	7 W	622/2568	3
Staffa Street	Just W of Leipzig Salient	7 W	624/2561	7
Stafford Avenue	NW of Gommecourt Park	7 W	621/2571	2
Standish Street	700m E of Ovillers Post	8 W	625/2558	8
Star Wood	1200m N of Serre	7 W	624/2569	3
Station Alley	N off Station Rd SE of B. Hamel	7 W	623/2564	5
Station Road	SE from Beaumont Hamel	7 W	623+/2564	5
Station Trench	Just S of Station Road	7 W	623/2564	5
Steinbruch Graben	Bet. La Bois. & Pozières on D929	8 E	626/2559	9
Steingraben	E from D929 NE of La Boisselle	8 E	627/2559	9
Strasburg Line	St. Pierre Div. to Schwaben Redoubt	7 W	624+/2562+	7
Stuff Redbout	3520m SE of fork on leaving B.Hamel S.	7 W	626/2563	7
Stuff Trench	N of Stuff Redoubt, Thiepval sector	7 W	626/2563	7
Stump Road	N from Regina Trench West	7 W	625/2563	7
Sudbury Trench	800m NW of Courcelette	7 E	628/2563	7

Site / Trench	Location	Map	Map Ref.	Obj.
Sunken Lane, Hawthorne Ridge	400m N of Hawthorne Mine Crater	7 W	6224/25657	5
Sunken Lane, Mansel Copse	Mansel Copse	8 E	6286/25546	12
Sunken Road - Fricourt Salient	Runs S from Crucifix Trench	8 E	627/2556	11
Sunken Road Trench – Mametz	Between Fricourt & Mametz	8 E	628+/2554	12
Sunken Road, Auchonvillers	Auchonvillers to Fabrique Farm	7 W	621/2565	5
Sunken Road, Scottish mem.	Runs N from Scottish memorial	7 W	622/2565	5
Switch Trench	Leipzig Salient	7 W	624/2561	7
Talus Boisé	1500m ENE of Carnoy	8 E	631/2554	14
Tara Hill	Just S of Bapaume Rd.before La Bois.	8 W	624/2557	9
Tara Redoubt	1500m SW of Y Sap crater	8 W	624/2557	9
Tarbert Street	Leipzig Salient	7 W	624/2561	7
Ten Tree Alley	Between Serre & Beaumont Hamel	7 W	623/2565+	5
Tenderloin Street	SSE from White City	7 W	622/2565	5
Thiepval Avenue	Authuille to Thiepval	7 W	624/2561	7
Thiepval Château	SW Thiepval	7 W	625/2562	7
Thiepval civil cemetery	Just N of Thiepval village	7 W	625/2562	7
Thiepval Fort	Thiepval village	7 W	625/2562	7
Thiepval plateau	see Thiepval ridge	7 W	625/2561+	7
Thiepval Ridge	N & SE of Thiepval	7 W	625/2561+	7
Thiepval Spur	see Thiepval Ridge	7 W	625/2561+	7
Thiepval village	4000m SE Beaumont Hamel	7 W	625/2562	7
Thorn Lane	900m WNW of Mametz Halt	8 E	627/2555	12
Thorpe Street	W of Gommecourt Park	7 W	621/2571	2
Thorsby Street	1700m NNE of Ovillers Post	8 E	625/2560	8
Thurles Dump	W of Y Ravine	7 W	622/2564	5
Thurso Road	Authuille village	7 W	624/2560	7
Thurso Street	Thiepval Wood	7 W	624/2562	7
Tipperary Avenue	W of Y Ravine	7 W	622/2564	5
Tirpitz Trench	900m SSW of Mametz	8 E	628/2554	12
Tithebarn Trench	Authuille-Ovillers road	7 W	624/2560	8
Tobermory Street	Just E of Authuille village	7 W	624/2560	7
Tollcross Street	Just E of Authuille village	7 W	624/2560	7
Tom's Cut	1100m SE of Mouquet Farm	7 E	627/2561	7
Toten Wald	see 257 Round Wood	8 E	6271/25572	10
Touvent Farm (new)	2.4km W Puisieux	7 W	623/2568	3
Touvent Farm (old - destroyed)	380m NNW Railway Hollow Cem.	7 W	622/2568	3
Train Alley	700m S of Montauban	8 E	631/2556	14
Transport Road	Between Sailly au Bois and Hébuterne	7 W	619+/2569	5
Triangle Point	500m N of Montauban	8 E	631/2557	14
Triangle, The	1200m NNW of Thiepval	7 W	6244/25629	7

Site / Trench	Location	Map	Map Ref.	Obj.
Triangle, The	ESE of Thiepval	7 W	625/2562	7
Triangle, The	Just E of New Munich Trench	7 W	624/25655	5
Triangle, The	700m SW of Pommiers Redoubt	8 E	629/2555	13
Triangle, The	800m NE of Scots Redoubt	8 E	627/2554	10
Triple Tambour Mine	500m W of Fricourt	8 E	6268/2556	11
Trongate	E of Thiepval Wood	7 W	624/2562	7
Twins, The	940m WSW of Montauban church	8 E	6309/25565	14
Tyler's Redboubt	Assembly position for attack on La Boisselle	8 E	626/2557	9
Tyndrum Street	Just W of Leipzig Salient	7 W	624/2561	7
Tyndrum Trench	Commun. T towards Leipzig Salient	7 W	624/2561	7
Ullmer Graben	WSW of Mouquet Farm	7 E	626/2561	7
Ulverstone Street	Just W of Ovillers	8 W	625/2559	8
Union Street	Thiepval Wood	7 W	624/2561+	7
Union Trench	1600m SSE of Mouquet Farm	7 E	627/2561	7
Ur Trench	560m N of Pigeon Wood	7 W	623/2573	2
Ural Trench	780m N of Pigeon Wood	7 W	623/2573	2
Usk Trench	550m N of Pigeon Wood	7 W	623/2572	2
Usna Hill	Just N. of Bapaume Rd.before La Bois.	8 W	624/2557	9
Usna Redoubt	1100m WSW of Y Sap crater	8 W	624/2558	9
Valley Avenue	W of Gommecourt Park	7 W	621/2571	2
Valley Trench	1600m ESE of Pommiers Redoubt	8 E	631/2555	14
Vercingetorix Trench	Cont. of Sackville Street	7 W	621/2568	3
W. Miraumont Rd	Runs S from Miraumont	7 E	628/2564+	5
Wagon Road	NNE from B.Hamel towards Serre	7 W	623/2565	5
Wagram Trench	W from Fort Sussex	7 W	621/2568	3
Walter Trench	W of Serre	7 W	624/2569	3
Waltney Street	1650m NNE of Ovillers Post	8 W	625/2560	8
Warren Trench	1300m ESE of Pommiers Redoubt	8 E	631/2555	14
Warrier Street	S of Gommecourt Park	7 W	621/2570	2
Waterloo Bridge	Bridge over trenches at Serre	7 W	622/2567	3
Watling Street	NW from B. Hamel to Serre Rd.	7 W	622/2566	5
Welcome Street	S of Gommecourt Park	7 W	621/2570	2
Wenning Street	Just S of Authuille Wood	8 W	624/2559	8
West Keep	250m W of Mound Keep	8 E	632/2554	14
Western Trench	900m SSE of Mouquet Farm	7 E	627/2560	7
Whalley Street	500m ENE of Ovillers Post	8 W	624/2558	8
Whiskey Street	S of Gommecourt Park	7 W	621/2570	2
Whisky Trench	550m SSW of Scots Redoubt	8 E	626/2557	10
Whitchurch Street	Thiepval Wood	7 W	624/2561+	7
White City	1300m NE of Auchonvillers	7 W	621+/2565	5
Whizzbang Avenue	NW of Gommecourt Park	7 W	621/2571	2
Wick Road	Authuille village	7 W	624/2560	7
Wicker Corner	200m W of Fricourt SW	8 E	626/2555	11
William Redan	1400m SSE of Y Ravine	7 W	623/2563	5
Willow Avenue	Just E of Fricourt	8 E	627/2555	12
Willow Patch	650m W of Shelter Wood	8 E	626/2557	11
Willow Stream	S Fricourt to Mametz Wood	8 E	627+/2555+	12

Site / Trench	Location	Map	Map Ref.	Obj.
Willow Trench	Fricourt S to Willow Avenue	8 E	627/2555	12
Wing Corner	600m SSW of Rose Cottage	8 E	627/2555	12
Wing Trench	Cont. of Flank Trench	7 W	625/2567	3
Wold Redoubt	500m W of Bailiff Wood	8 E	627/2558	10
Wolf Trench	Between Beaumont Hamel & Serre	7 W	623/2565+	5
Woman Street	S of Gommecourt Park	7 W	621/2570	2
Wonder Werk	800m S of Thiepval	7 W	625/2561	7
Wood Alley	Immed. S of Scots Redoubt	8 E	627/2557	9
Wood Post	1970m S of Thiepval	8 W	624/2559	7
Wood Street	S of Gommecourt Park	7 W	621/2570	2
Worcester Trench	1170m W of Pozières	8 E	626/2560	7
Word Work	Between Pozières & Leipzig Salient	7 E	626/2560	7
Worley Trench	S of Matthew Copse	7 W	622/2567	3
Wundt Werk	1000m E of Pendant Copse	7 W	625/2567	5
Wurzel Street	S of Gommecourt Park	7 W	621/2570	2
Y Ravine	640m S of Beaumont Hamel church	7 W	622/2564	5
Y Sap Mine	N side of main road at La Boisselle	8 W	6254/25585	9
Y Street	400m SW of Hawthorne Crater	7 W	622/2565	5
Yankee Street	S of Gommecourt Park	7 W	621/2570	2
Yankee Trench	700m S of Gommecourt Park	7 W	621/2570	5
Yatman, Bridge	Bridge over Ancre N of Authuille	7 W	624/2560	7
Yellow Line	Brit. defences after 2nd att. on Serre	7 W	622/2567+	3
Yellow Street	S of Gommecourt Park	7 W	621/2570	2
Yiddish Street	S of Commecourt Park	7 W	621/2570	2
Young Street	S of Gommecourt Park	7 W	621/2570	2
Yussuf Street	S of Gommecourt Park	7 W	621/2570	2
Z Salient	N of Gommecourt Wood	7 W	622/2572	2
Z, The	Just N of Gommecourt Wood	7 W	621/2571	2
Zahringer Graben	500m E of Lochnagar crater	8 E	626/2557	9
Zigzag Trench	Just W of Mouquet Farm	7 E	626/2561	7
Zinc Trench	900m of Mametz Halt	8 E	627/2555	12
Zollern Graben	W of Courcelette	7 E	627+/2562	7
Zollern Redbout	1200m N of Mouquet Farm	7 E	6265/25629	7
Zollern Trench, Thiepval	E of château d'eau, Thiepval	7 W	6257/25624	7

Alphabetical List of locations situated generally behind the Front Line

Site / Place	Location	Map	Map Ref.
Acheux-en-Amienois	8.8km W Beaumont Hamel	7 W	614/2564
Auchonvillers	1.9km W Beaumont Hamel	7 W	621/2564
Authuille	4.5km S Beaumont Hamel	7 W	623/2560
Aveluy	2.4km N Albert	8 W	623/2558
Baizieux	9km WSW Albert	8 W	613/2555
Bayencourt	4.4km WSW Foncquevillers	7 W	617/2570
Beauquesne GHQ	20km NW of Albert	52	Fold 8
Beaussart	5.3km W Beaumont Hamel	7 W	617/2565
Bécordel-Bécourt	2.8km ESE Albert	8 W	625/2555
Bécourt	2.8km E Albert	8 W	625/2556
Bécourt Wood (Fr. Bois Planté)	3km E of Albert	8 W	625/2555
Bertrancourt	7km W Beaumont Hamel	7 W	616/2566
Bienvillers au Bois	4.3km NNW Gommecourt	7 W	620/2575
Blighty Valley- formerly Nab Valley	S of Leipzig Salient	7 W	624/2560
Bois Brulé	900 WSW Hardecourt aux Bois	8 E	633/2554
Bois Caffet	200m SW Carnoy	8 E	629/2554
Bois Carré	900m SSW Hardecourt aux Bois	8 E	634/2554
Bois Choque	1.7km SSE Carnoy	8 E	630/2552
Bois Dauvillers	SW of Mailly-Maillet	7 W	617+/2563+
Bois d'Aveluy	S of Mesnil-Martinsart	7 W	622+/2560+
Bois de Billon	1.5km S Carnoy	8 E	630/2552
Bois de Sailly	1000m W of Sailly au Bois	7 W	617/2569
Bois d'en Haut	600m S Hardecourt aux Bois	8 E	634/2554
Bois d'Engrement	1km S Fricourt	8 E	627/2554
Bois des Bus	Just N of Bus les Artois	7 W	614/2568
Bois Favier	900m W Hardecourt aux Bois	8 E	633/2555
Bois Futaie	NW of Englebelmer	7 W	618/2563+
Bois Hédauville	SE of Hédauville	7 W	617/2560
Bois St. Gauchy	600m SE Carnoy	8 E	630/2554
Bosquet, le	Just S of Colincamps	7 W	618/2566
Bouzincourt	3.4km NW Albert	8 W	619/2558
Box Wood	1300m N of Serre	7 W	624/2569
Bray-sur-Somme	6.4km S Fricourt	8 E	627/2549
Bresle	6.8km WSW Albert	8 W	616/2554
Buire-sur-Ancre	6.1km SW Albert	8 W	618/2552
Bus-les-Artois	8.5km WNW Beaumont Hamel	7 W	614/2567
Caftet Wood	500m SW of Carnoy	8 E	629/2554
Cappy village	SE of Bray sur Somme	8 E	630/2547
Carnoy	SE of Fricourt	8 E	630/2554

Site / Place	Location	Map	Map Ref.
Cerisy	10.5km S Albert	8 W	621/2545
Chipilly village	SW of Bray sur Somme	8 W	622/2545
Coigneux	6km WSW Foncquevillers	7 W	615/2570
Colincamps	4.3km NW Beaumont Hamel	7 W	619/2567
Couin	7.3km WSW Foncquevillers	7 W	613/2570
Courcelles au Bois	5.7km NW Beaumont Hamel	7 W	617/2567
Dernancourt	3.4km SSW Albert	8 W	621/2553
Englebelmer	4.5km SW Beaumont Hamel	7 W	619/2562
Etinehem	8.8km SSE Albert	8 W	625/2547
Farm, Bronfay	2km SSW Carnoy	8 E	629/2552
Farm, de la Haie	2.9km WSW Foncquevillers	7 W	618/2571
Farm, du Billon	1.4km S Carnoy	8 E	629/2552
Farm, du Bois de Branlé	600m E Colincamps	7 W	619/2567
Farm, du Bois de Quesnoy	3.5km E Hannescamps	7 W	625/2574
Farm, la Fabrique	2km ESE Colincamps	7 W	620/2566
Farm, la Signy	2.3km W Serre	7 W	621/2567
Farm, Pierrard	2km SW Puisieux	7 W	623/2568
Foncquevillers	1.3km NW Gommecourt	7 W	621/2572
Forceville	7.5km WSW Beaumont Hamel	7 W	615/2562
Fort Anley	S of Auchonvillers	7 W	621/2564
Fort Briggs	WNW of Serre	7 W	622/2568
Fort Southdown (Wagram)	WNW of Serre	7 W	621/2568
Fort Sussex	WNW of Serre	7 W	621/2568
Garenne Blanche	1.6 km SSW Maricourt	8 E	631/2552
Garenne de la Grosse Tête	2200m SW Maricourt	8 E	631/2552
Garenne de Maricourt	2600m SSW Maricourt	8 E	631/2551
Garenne des Malvaux	1.6 km SW Maricourt	8 E	631/2552
Garenne des Muterlets	1.6 km WSW Maricourt	8 E	631/2553
Garenne du Moulin	1200m WSW Maricourt	8 E	631/2553
Garenne du Vicaire	1 km SW of Maricourt	8 E	631/2553
Hamelet	13.8km SW Albert	8 W	613/2545
Hannescamps	3km N Gommecourt	7 W	621/2574
Happy Valley	Opp. Peronne Rd. Cem. at Maricourt	8 E	631/2553
Hébuterne	3.2km NW Serre	7 W	621/2569
Hédauville	7.5km SW Beaumont Hamel	7 W	616/2561
Heilly	9.55km SW Albert	8 W	614/2550
Héne	7.3km W Foncquevillers	7 W	613/2573
Hénencourt	6km W Albert	8 W	616/2556
Hubercamps	7.2km NW Gommecourt	7 W	616/2576
La Guerre Wood	500m S of Carnoy	8 E	630/2553
La Prée Wood	600m SE of Carnoy	8 E	630/2553
Lancashire Dump	On site of Aveluy Wood Brit. Cem.	7 W	623/2561
Laviéville	5.4km WSW Albert	8 W	617/2555
Le Hamel	13km SW Albert	8 W	616/2544

Site / Place	Location	Map	Map Ref.
Louvencourt	14km NW of Albert		IGNNo.4, fold 2
Ludgate Circus	1840m W of Carnoy	8 E	629/2554
Mailly-Maillet	3.8km W Beaumont Hamel	7 W	619/2564
Maple Redoubt	1080m WSW of Mansel Copse	8 E	627/2554
Maricourt village	E of Carnoy	8 E	632/2553
Martinsart	5km SSW Beaumont Hamel	7 W	621/2560
Méaulte	2.6km S Albert	8 W	623/2554
Méricourt l'Abbe	8.4km SW Albert	8 W	616/2550
Méricourt sur Somme	10.5km SSE Albert	8 W	624/2545
Mesnil Ridge	N of Mesnil towards Hamel	7 W	622/2562
Mesnil-Martinsart	3.4km S Beaumont Hamel	7 W	622/2562
Millencourt	4.5km W Albert	8 W	617/2556
Minden Post	800m SW of Carnoy	8 E	629/2553
Monchy-au-Bois	4.6km NNE Gommecourt	7 W	623/2576
Montreuil	General GHQ before Somme offensive		
Morlancourt	6km S Albert	8 W	621/2550
Observation Wood	W of Matthew Copse	7 W	623/2567
One Tree Hill	E of Kilometer Lane	7 W	622/2566
Park Lane	Joins Ration Trench to OG1	7 E	627/2561
Pommier	6km NW Gommecourt	7 W	618/2576
Querrieu, Château de, GHQ	17km towards Amiens from Albert	52	Pli 8
Ribemont sur Ancre	7.8km SW Albert	8 W	616/2551
Rostrum Trench	N of Auchonvillers	7 W	621/2565
Sailly-au-Bois	6.1km NW Beaumont Hamel	7 W	618/2569
Sailly-Laurette	10.6km SSW Albert	8 W	619/2546
Sailly-le-Sec	11km SW Albert	8 W	617/2547
Senlis-le-Sec	5.8km NW Albert	8 W	617/2559
Souastre	4.7km W Foncquevillers	7 W	616/2573
St. Amand	6.8km WNW Gommecourt	7 W	616/2574
Sugar Factory	NW of the Bowery	7 W	622/2566
Thiepval Wood	1300 SE of monument at Hamel	7 W	624/2562
Treux	6.7km SW Albert	8 W	618/2551
Vaire-sous-Corbie	12.5km SW Albert	8 W	615/2546
Varennes	9.5km WSW Beaumont Hamel	7 W	614/2561
Vaux sur Somme	12km SW Albert	8 W	615/2547
Ville sur Ancre	5.5km SSW Albert	8 W	619/2551
Villers-Bretonneux	19km SW Albert	8 W	613/2541
Vitermont	3.8km SW Beaumont Hamel	7 W	619/2563
Warloy-Baillon	9km WNW Albert	8 W	613/2557
Wellington Redoubt	1800m W of Carnoy	8 E	629/2554
White Trench	500m SE of tip of Mametz Wood	8 E	629/2557

ONE DAY ON THE SOMME

THE ATTACKS

Having established the statistics behind the Battle of the Somme, we now come to the details surrounding each attack on the specific objectives. To assist the reader, each attack has been dealt with individually, and the reader will find for each of the objectives:-

A map of the area showing the lines of attack of the various infantry battalions engaged.
Where possible, the trenches mentioned in the text are marked on the maps.
In a few cases, one map covers two objectives where these are adjacent.

Details of the division, brigades and battalions engaged.

An account of the action.

The British Military Cemetery at Authuille, set on a steep slope running down to the River Ancre. Situated in lovely countryside but a little way from the main road, it does not have the same number of visitors as the larger, well-known cemeteries, but is one the author often visits

Objective 2

The Gommecourt Diversion

Battalions Engaged

Corps	Div.	Brig.	Bn.No.	Battalion
VII	46	137	5	South Staffs
VII	46	137	6	South Staffs
VII	46	137	5	North Staffs
VII	46	137	6	North Staffs
VII	46	138	4	Lincolns
VII	46	138	5	Lincolns
VII	46	138	4	Leicesters
VII	46	138	5	Leicesters
VII	46	139	5	Sherwood Foresters
VII	46	139	6	Sherwood Foresters
VII	46	139	7	Sherwood Foresters, Robin Hood Rifles
VII	46	139	8	Sherwood Foresters
VII	46	0	1	Monmouths (pioneers)
VII	56	167	1	London
VII	56	167	3	London
VII	56	167	7	Middlesex
VII	56	167	8	Middlesex
VII	56	168	4	London
VII	56	168	12	London - Rangers
VII	56	168	13	London - Kensington
VII	56	168	14	London - 1st London Scottish
VII	56	169	2	London
VII	56	169	5	London - 1st London Rifle Brigade
VII	56	169	9	London - Queen Victoria's Rifles
VII	56	169	16	London - Queen's Westminster Rifles
VII	56	0	5	Cheshires (pioneers)

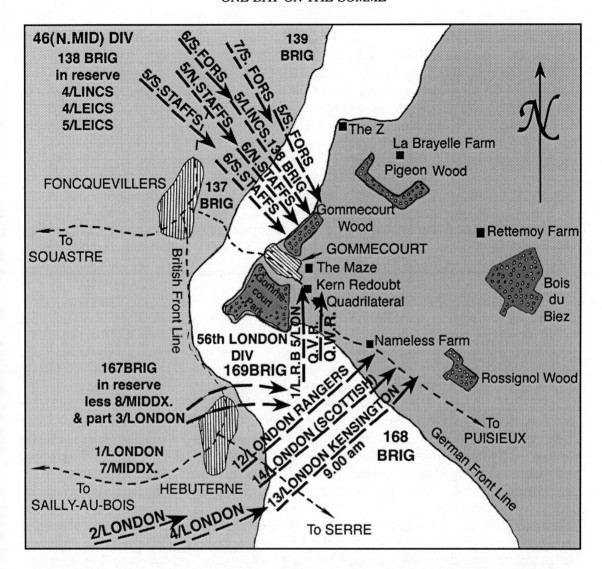

General Sir E. Allenby's Third Army was at the extreme north of the British front line in the Somme area on the 1st July. All units south of Gommecourt were part of General Sir H. Rawlinson's Fourth Army. General Sir Douglas Haig was the Commander in Chief of both armies although it was Rawlinson who, in discussion with Haig, conceived the general plan of attack for the whole campaign.

The Third Army was to make a diversionary attack on the Gommecourt Salient. A two-mile gap separated this sector from the 31st Division at Serre. Having no British units immediately to the north, both flanks would be exposed with no possibility of reinforcement.

Its VII Corps had three divisions, the 46th (North Midland), the 56th (London) and the 37th, the latter holding the front line some distance to the north. The two divisions took over the area at the beginning of May, giving them little time to prepare for the attack. Following an unsuccessful attack on the Salient by the French in 1915, the Germans had since made their defences even stronger. It was not of great importance to Haig if the salient was not taken. The task of the VII Corps was to *"...assist in the operations of the Fourth Army by diverting against itself the fire of artillery and infantry which might otherwise be directed against the left flank of the main attack near Serre"* [Official History, page 454]. For this reason, the Corps Commander, Lieut.-Gen. T. Snow advised the two divisional commanders to fulfil the diversionary requirements but not to press home attacks on Gommecourt until the German defences had been destroyed. But this was impossible, the enemy dugouts were up to forty feet deep. The ground was soft and muddy leaving insufficient time to mine the German defences. No Man's Land was up to 750 meters facing the 56th Division and around 450 meters for the 46th Division. Trenches had to be prepared. No labour corps was in the area and the trenches had to be dug by the infantry and pioneers. It was arduous work digging in the muddy ground and the men laboured continuously until the eve of the attack.

The village of Gommecourt lay on the northern edge of Gommecourt Park, a large wood with the German front line running the whole length of its southern and western fringes. Gommecourt Wood lay to the north of the village on the right of the German front line. Both woods, although much damaged by the long barrage, offered perfect spots to hide machine guns. Attacking infantry would have to overcome the immense problem of scrambling over abattis and other natural impediments of a tangled wood with trenches in all directions. In view of these difficulties, it was decided not to make a frontal attack on the salient but to make two flanking movements, the 46th Division to attack from the north west and the 56th from the south west - the two divisions to link up some 700 meters east of Gommecourt, thereby isolating the salient.

The attack had been originally planned for June 28th but heavy rain caused a postponement of two days. Meanwhile, for three nights the 56th Division had put 3,000 men in No Man's Land, their sector not being quite so water-soaked, to reduce its width by digging a trench. This incredible achievement was carried out by the Royal Engineers, 5/Cheshires (Pioneers) and infantry from the 167th Brigade. Although the Germans were well aware of the activities, the casualties were remarkably low. For the 46th Division, which had suffered many casualties through German shelling, the problem was not so much the width of No Man's Land but the muddy conditions in the trenches. In places the men were up to their knees in water. In front lay a mass of barbed wire left by the French. After tremendous exertions a shallow trench was dug into No Man's Land but this too, filled with water. The only course left was to crawl out towards the German front line a few minutes before the British barrage was lifted.

The 37th Division to the north was to place a barrage in its own sector accompanied by machine gun and Stokes mortar fire to induce the Germans to think another separate attack was imminent. This, along with the flagrantly obvious preparations at Gommecourt did serve a useful purpose, the enemy diverting a division with its artillery to the Gommecourt sector.

The 137th and 139th Brigades of the 46th Division were assembled facing Gommecourt Wood. The 6/South Staffs and 6/North Staffs led the 137th Brigade with the Staffords of the 5th North and South in support. The 5/Lincolns attached from 138th Brigade was in reserve. To their left the 139th Brigade was led by the 5th and 7th Sherwood Foresters, the 6th in support and the 8th in Brigade reserve. The remaining three battalions of the 138th Brigade were in divisional reserve. Each of the assault brigades had an attachment of Royal Engineers. The 5/Monmouth (Pioneers) had the unpleasant task of improving and digging the trenches.

The 137th began their attack under cover of a smoke screen so dense that some men lost their way causing gaps in the planned attack formations. However, the screen dissipated fairly quickly and the advance across the muddy ground continued. The Staffords were only half way across No Man's Land, held up by wire twisted and damaged but not cut, when the Germans were out of the dug-outs and mounting the machine guns. At the same time the enemy laid an intense bombardment on No-Man's-Land forcing the Staffords to take cover. Machine gun fire from the German strongpoint "The Z", just north of Gommecourt Wood prevented any movement of the rear companies of the leading and support battalions. The 6th South and 6th North Staffords reached the wire where they were cut down by machine gun fire and hand grenades. Just a few reached the front line where, without support, they were driven out, killed or wounded.

The 139th Brigade on the left of the 137th was composed entirely of Sherwood Foresters, The leading companies of the 5th and 7th had crawled partly into No Man's Land. At 7.30am they rushed and took the first German trench at considerable cost and some continued towards the second line. As soon as the British barrage lifted, the remaining Germans emerged from the dug-outs, mounted their guns separating the leading companies from the support waves. The fate of the 5th and 7th Sherwood Foresters was sealed. The German barrage on No Man's Land prevented any possibility of support getting through. The following waves, not having any element of surprise, suffered terrible casualties in No Man's Land. Later waves could not get forward at all.

By 9.00am it was evident the 137th Brigade's attack had failed. 139th Brigade had made a lodgement in the front line and was in desperate need of support. This was desperately urgent as the 56th Division to the south had made good progress as will be seen later. However, in spite of various plans and attempts to reorganise the support and reserve battalions, the difficulties of organisation, ground conditions and the immense problem of effective and accurate communication resulted in the plans having to be aborted. The only possible solution was to attack again with entirely fresh troops but there were none available at Gommecourt.

The 168th and 169th Brigades of the 56th Division were south of Gommecourt village, the 167th Brigade less the 8/Middlesex and half the 3/London being in reserve to the north of Hébuterne. Each of the assault brigades had specific objectives, the 168th, the

The line of attack of the 46th (North Midland) Division towards the western edge of Gommecourt Wood.

German third trench Fame-Felon. The 169th was to approach Gommecourt cemetery via Fell-Fellow-Freud trenches, then swing left towards the Quadrilateral and beyond to link up with the 46th Division.

The 12th and 14th London led the 168th Brigade supported by the 4/London while the 5th and 9th London, supported by the 16/London with the 2/London in reserve made up the 169th Brigade. The attack by both brigades was made with great valour and determination. At 7.30am under cover of a smoke screen they dashed forward, passed through the wire which was reasonably cut and were in the front line trench before the Germans had time to react. They continued and took the second and third trenches, the latter only after a hard struggle. They had now achieved their first objective. Nameless Farm in the path of the 12/London Rangers was not taken. Although completely in ruins, its cellars and the ruins themselves provided good positions for machine gun and rifle fire.

In spite of the German barrage, the support battalions moved forward and the gains of the leading battalions were consolidated. Of about 300 German prisoners sent back, nearly a quarter were killed by their own barrage. The support battalion, the Queen's Westminsters now moved forward to take the Quadrilateral. A party of bombers approached up Freud Trench from the cemetery but all were killed or wounded. The remaining companies of the assault and support battalions were pinned down by a most effective barrage from No Man's Land to the front trenches. Numerous efforts were made to carry up bombs and ammunition but the carrying parties were destroyed. German counter attacks thinned the line of the 168th and 169th Brigades. Shortly after 9.00am a party of 13/London Kensington with a machine gun crew of the London Scottish managed to reach the remainder of the London Scottish. In spite of heroic efforts later in the day, no more reinforcements were to get through. The position of the assault battalions was quickly becoming untenable and, by mid afternoon, out of bombs and having used all the stick-grenades found in the German trenches, they were forced back from the third line.

Attempts were made by the men who could not get forward to bring in some of the hundreds of wounded laying in No Man's Land. There was a temporary truce, the Germans permitting recovery on the British side of the wire on condition of a cessation of fire. Most unfortunately, the truce was broken when an 18 pounder shelled the German front trench - possibly due to lack of communication.

At 2.00pm the two brigades had retreated to the second line but were still holding the trench and the southern part of Gommecourt Park. Only the intervention by the 46th Division could save the situation, but all was quiet, their attack having failed. The news came up from Serre that the attack of the 31st Division had failed, the German artillery there now free to help guns from Puisieux and elsewhere. Two hours later, the courageous Londoners had been forced back to the first line.

The division still had two and a half fairly fresh battalions and the 46th Division a further three and a half. Plans were made for them to help the VIII Corps to the south but were later aborted.

Facing an increasing number of German counter attacks the Londoners were now being forced back to the wire. Incredibly they held on, almost out of ammunition. At dark, the last of their bullets expended, they retired to their starting point suffering very heavy casualties.

In the 46th Division, a last effort was made to make contact with the men supposedly hanging on in the enemy trench. - most, in fact, were lying wounded in No Man's Land.

After midnight the 5/Lincoln and 5/Leicester on the right flank went forward to find the Germans still very much on the alert. German flares revealed their position and they took what cover they could find. On receiving the order to retire the Lincolns brought in at considerable cost many of the wounded.

As dawn broke the following day the Germans opposite the 46th Division placed a red-cross flag on the parapet. Both German and British collected their wounded. A German aeroplane dropped a list of prisoners taken during the battle. The British reciprocated the gesture two days later.

The 56th (London) Division had achieved all its objectives and had put up a fine show. Unfortunately, the 46th Division's attack was doomed to failure right from the start and was not able to give any support to the Londoners. It had been a costly affair, and the Diversion which was to attract enemy fire had resulted in 2,455 casualties in the 46th Division and 4,314 in the 56th. It could be said the Diversion had achieved its aim in that German troops and artillery had been transferred to the area thus diverting fire from the Fourth Army. But the loss of nearly seven thousand men did not help the Pals attack on Serre as will be seen in the next section.

Objective 3

Serre

Battalions Engaged

Corps	Div.	Brig.	Bn.No.	Battalion
VIII	31	92	10	East Yorks - Hull Commercials
VIII	31	92	11	East Yorks - Hull Tradesmen
VIII	31	92	12	East Yorks - Hull Sportsmen
VIII	31	92	13	East Yorks - T'Others
VIII	31	93	15	West Yorks - Leeds Pals
VIII	31	93	16	West Yorks - 1st Bradford Pals
VIII	31	93	18	West Yorks - 2nd Bradford Pals
VIII	31	93	18	Durham Light Infantry - Durham Pals
VIII	31	94	11	East Lancs - Accrington Pals
VIII	31	94	12	Yorks and Lancs - Sheffield City Battalion
VIII	31	94	13	Yorks and Lancs - 1st Barnsley Pals
VIII	31	94	14	Yorks and Lancs - 2nd Barnsley Pals
VIII	31	0	12	K.O.Y.L.I. Halifax Pals (Pioneers)

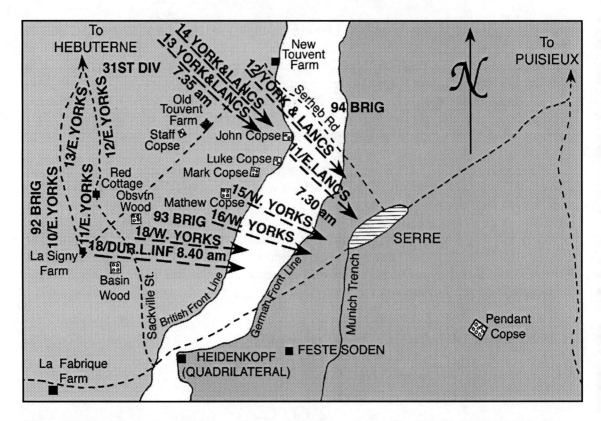

The village of Serre-Lez-Puisieux, known simply as Serre, lies on the D919, 1900 meters south west of Puisieux. The Germans had been in this sector since late 1914 and had had ample time to prepare good fortifications and chose the high ground for their artillery emplacements giving the gunners an excellent view over a wide area. By early 1915 the German line followed a northerly line west of Serre along which Touvent Farm formed a well fortified salient.

In May 1915 the French army was under pressure north of Arras on the Lorette and Vimy ridges and it was decided their Second Army under General de Castelnau would make a diversionary attack at Serre to prevent German reinforcements being sent north from the Hébuterne area. The first task facing the French was to straighten the German line by taking the salient at Touvent Farm. From the 7th to the 13th June the French made four desperate and courageous attacks and took the first and second German trenches. Finally, Touvent Farm salient was wrested from the Germans and the reformed Allied line 500 meters east of Touvent Farm augured well for a subsequent attack on Serre. It was de Castelnau's wish to continue the attack from the new line but the French were exhausted and their ranks too depleted. This "diversion" had cost 11,000 French casualties. The sector became calm with only desultory firing from either side. In April 1916, the British 31st Division took over the line from the French.

A necessary but onerous task facing the men of the 31st Division on their arrival was the reorganisation of their front line position. Trenches were repaired and extended and the many hundreds of French dead found in shallow graves were given a decent burial. The division had arrived in France after duty in Egypt at the Suez Canal. It was composed of the 92nd, 93rd and 94th Brigades plus a battalion of pioneers, the 12/K.O.Y.L.I. This was a unique division in the New Army in that it was composed entirely of Pals battalions, men from Durham, Yorkshire, Lancashire and Hull. Whole groups of men from factories, offices, shops, banks, mines, etc had volunteered en masse in Kitchener's New Army. There was a camaraderie amongst these men who had worked together in peacetime and who had decided to fight together for the Just Cause on the Somme. It was something entirely new and which was never to be seen again.

The objective of the 31st Division was to take Serre at the northern end of the British line and to pivot in a wide arc to protect the British divisions to the south. The 94th Brigade was to attack Serre from the north west and the leading battalions were situated in front of John Copse with the support battalions behind the copse. The 93rd Brigade was in position to the east of Observation Wood and the reserve brigade, the 92nd, was north of La Signy Farm.

Serre was only a small village and to all appearances should not have presented a major problem to the attacking infantry. But since the French attack in June 1915, the Germans had completed extensive repairs and amelioration to their defence system. It is possible the British High Command was aware of this but there was high confidence in the effectiveness of the week-long bombardment in the last week of June 1916. Rawlinson was confident that the wire would be well cut and the German dug-outs destroyed.

The sheer noise of the bombardment must have given heart to the waiting infantry. How could anything survive? No Man's Land was about 300 yards wide and the 12/K.O.Y.L.I. pioneers had been holding the front line and, while waiting for the leading battalions to take up their positions, had suffered many casualties during patrols and wire cutting sorties. The bulk of the pioneers were withdrawn to an area near La Signy Farm but some were detailed to reinforce the Durham and Accrington Pals in the initial attack. Forward saps had been dug to lessen the width of No Man's Land. At 7.20am on the 1st July the great mine on the Hawthorn Ridge, 2800 meters west south west of Serre was blown and the VIII Corps heavy artillery lifted its barrage. The Germans, on hearing the explosion on the Hawthorn Ridge, realised an attack was imminent. For some while also, the enemy had been shelling the British front line and support positions with a selection of their artillery. It will be remembered the artillery had an excellent overview of the whole of the British positions and there were many British casualties before the main attack began. At 7.30am precisely, the whistles were heard throughout the whole line and the leading battalions left their saps to advance on the first line of German trenches. The artillery barrage lengthened its range in accordance with the carefully laid plans so that it would always be just in front of the advancing infantry. Events were to prove that the infantry was not able to keep to the plan of advance and, therefore, the British artillery, which was allowed no deviation to the plan, was ranged on targets which were of no help to the struggling infantry battalions. These hardy men from the north of England were at last to have the chance to fight the Hun. As soon as they were in No Man's Land, the Germans laid a precise barrage on this deadly area and although the wire was partially cut, there were stretches where the infantry was desperately struggling with their small wire cutters to clear a way through the wire. The German machine gunners had come up from their deep dugouts, no longer troubled by the British artillery, and could not believe the sight before their eyes. Wave after of wave of heavily laden men were advancing as

The leading battalions of the 94th brigade, 31st Division attacked Serre from this point, the Accrington Pals and the Sheffield City battalions suffering heavy losses. The photograph was taken in Sheffield Park, looking down towards the British Support Trenches and Railway Hollow British Military Cemetery.

though on parade. They were a perfect target for the machine guns, some gunners even standing on top of the parapet to fire more effectively.

The Sheffield City Battalion and the Accrington Pals of the 94th Brigade advanced through a hail of steel and fell in their hundreds. A few of the two leading battalions reached the first enemy trench. British observers anxiously trying to evaluate the progress of the infantry reported that some 80 to 100 men, possibly a mixture of 12/Yorks and Lancs and 11/E Lancs, were seen to be entering the village of Serre. This news spread like wildfire and soon reports of the imminent capture of Serre was in the British newspapers. But these few gallant men were never seen again. The bodies of some 12/Yorks & Lancs were found in the north west corner of Serre during a later attack in November. At 7.35am the two support battalions of the 94th Brigade, the 13 and 14/Yorks and Lancs were ordered forward to support the failing attack of their comrades but as soon as they entered No Man's Land, the German artillery laid a heavy barrage which decimated the ranks of the Barnsley Pals and their dead lay in the cratered ground.

The 93rd Brigade was to suffer the same fate. The Leeds Pals had lost heavily in the formation trenches before the attack began and those who were able to venture into No Man's Land never got through the wire. The 1st Bradford Pals endured the same obstacles with the same horrendous consequences. They too were cut down. The sight of the vast number of dead facing the support battalions of the Bradford and Durham Pals as they began their attack at 8.40am is almost too sad to contemplate. But advance they did, with great resolution as if to avenge the death of their friends, but they also, were destined to fall in their hundreds. A small number of the Durham Pals somehow continued through the screen of bullet and shell and, in ever decreasing numbers, continued as far as Pendant Copse. Like their comrades who had entered Serre, the few Durham Pals were never seen again.

There had been no hesitation or lack of determination in the attack. The men had come through their baptism of fire with great courage. Most died in the first hundred yards of the attack. The losses belie belief and it was evident by mid morning the attack had failed. The commanders took the decision not to commit the 92nd Brigade and it remained in reserve apart from some of the Hull Commercials (10/E Yorks) who were sent forward to help the pioneer battalion repair the battered defences and help the wounded.

As the firing died down on either side the air was filled with the lament of the wounded and dying. The wounded tried to find shelter in some hollow or crater, hardly daring to move for fear of being hit by a German sniper. They were soon out of water and had to pass the long day in the hot sun. Many died from their wounds. As darkness fell, the task of clearing No Man's Land began. The dead and wounded were brought in - many of the dead could not be identified. Three days were to pass before most of the casualties were brought in. A large number of corpses still hung on the wire and it was not possible to recover these bodies until the spring of 1917.

The total casualties of the 93rd & 94th Brigades and the pioneers were 3600, that is to say, an average loss of 400 for each of the nine battalions. Four battalions had casualties in excess of 500; the worst hit being the Accrington Pals with 585, the Leeds Pals, 1st Bradford Pals and the Sheffield City Battalion having between 510 and 530 casualties each.

The day which promised so much had ended in tragedy. In less than an hour the Pals battalions of the 94th and 93rd Brigades had been virtually destroyed. It is difficult to imagine the trauma of the roll calls that evening. The War Office later forbade large groups of volunteers from the same local area to join the same battalion as public reaction, once the enormous casualty lists were published, began to protest against the human sacrifice on the Somme and people were starting to ask if the war was being conducted in the best possible way.

In spite of super-human efforts by both infantry and artillery, the village of Serre was never taken by the Allies. There was a further attack in November but that too, failed and the British only entered the village after the voluntary evacuation by the Germans to their newly prepared Hindenberg Line early in 1917.

The Accrington Pals Memorial in Sheffield Park, Serre.

Objective 4
South of Serre & North of Beaumont Hamel

Battalions Engaged

Corps	Div.	Brig.	Bn.No.	Battalion
VIII	4	10	2	Royal Dublin Fusiliers
VIII	4	10	1	Royal Irish Fusiliers
VIII	4	10	1	Royal Warwicks
VIII	4	10	2	Seaforth Highlanders
VIII	4	11	1	East Lancs
VIII	4	11	1	Hampshires
VIII	4	11	1	Rifle Brigade
VIII	4	11	1	Somerset Light Infantry
VIII	4	12	2	Duke of Wellington's
VIII	4	12	2	Essex
VIII	4	12	1	King's Own
VIII	4	12	2	Lancs Fusiliers
VIII	4	143	8	Royal Warwicks - attached from 48th Div.
VIII	4	143	6	Royal Warwicks - attached from 48th Div.
VIII	4	0	21	West Yorks (pioneers)

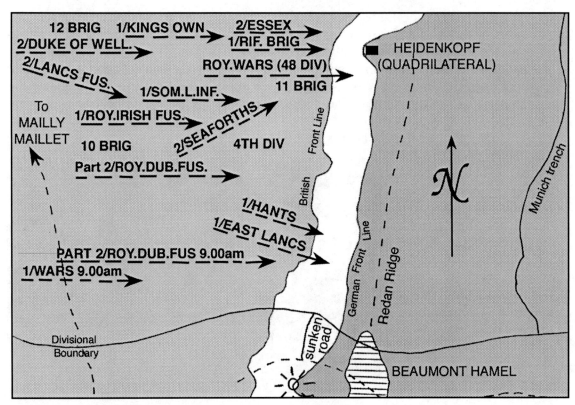

The area covered by the attack of the 4th Division was the Heidenkopf, also known as the Quadrilateral Redoubt, a German strongpoint 1600 meters south west of Serre. To the south of the redoubt the objectives were the Redan Ridge and east towards Munich Trench. There were no villages in the day's objectives, no names which elsewhere were to become household names, but just the hard task of attacking the German defences in this barren sector. These men were regular soldiers of the original British Expeditionary Force (B.E.F.) and were considered to be at the peak of fitness and training.

The 11th Brigade, reinforced by the 6 & 8/Royal Warwicks attached from the 48th Division, was to attack the Heidenkopf and the enemy second line. Then, the 10th and 12th Brigades were to pass through the gains and take the German third line. Reports from our observation posts were encouraging, the wire seemed to be well cut and the front line enemy trenches destroyed. What was not known at this time was that the deep German dug outs, although severely pounded, were nevertheless, still largely intact, many having numerous entry and exit points.

At 7.20am when the Hawthorn Mine was exploded and the heavy artillery lifted its barrage, the whole British front line came under heavy machine gun and artillery fire. The three forward battalions of the 11th Brigade were in split trenches in No Man's Land and suffered heavily from enemy fire as did the support battalions waiting for the order to advance. It was a formidable task facing the men at zero hour, ten minutes later. The 1/E Lancs and the 1/Rifle Brigade suffered severe losses. The wire was indeed well cut and the first enemy trenches were reached and a few men reached their objective, the second line but, here, they could not hold. The left company of the Rifle Brigade advanced with the Royal Warwicks, entered the Heidenkopf and a support trench to the rear of the redoubt but here, they came under heavy fire from Serre, the attack just to the north by the 31st Division having failed there.

At 7.40am the support battalions moved forward across the cratered ground still under heavy bombardment. The 1/Hants and the 1/S.L.I. moved forward from one shell hole to the next but were unable to reach the German front line, so intense was the enemy fire power. The same fire forced the 1/S.L.I. to veer away from their planned line of attack but the battalion was able to reinforce the Royal Warwicks and the Rifle Brigade in the Heidenkopf. The 6/Royal Warwicks moved forward to support its sister battalion but it, too, came under flank fire from Serre.

The news from the Heidenkopf was good but there were large numbers of men unable to move in No Man's Land on their attack on the Redan Ridge. An order was issued to halt the attack but this was not received in time by the 10th Brigade and the 2/Royal Dublin Fusiliers moved forward to suffer the same fate as their comrades. The 2/Seaforth Highlanders along with two companies of the 2/Lancs Fusiliers of the 12th Brigade were, like the S.L.I. forced to veer left and abandon their original line of attack and they reinforced the other battalions at the Heidenkopf.

Some troops had reached Munich Trench which runs south from Serre and were reinforced by the 1/King's Own and the 2/Essex and were thus able to continue as far as Pendant Copse - a remarkable feat under the intense enemy fire. However, the inevitable German counter attacks forced the men to abandon these gains and they were driven back to the Heidenkopf where a further counter attack was feared. The 2/Duke of Wellington's were sent forward in support but it was impossible to get bombs and ammunition through to the redoubt. The Heidenkopf was held throughout the day but aggressive enemy counter attacks forced our troops to abandon this gain about noon the following day.

And so, in the end, the advance had failed and the infantry found themselves back in their own trenches. There are several reasons for this failure. Firstly, the premature detonation of the Hawthorn Mine before zero hour which allowed the German machine gunners to prepare their guns before the main advance at 7.30am, secondly, the commanding position of the German artillery and finally, the failure of the attacks by the 31st Division to the north and the 29th Division to the south resulted in the 4th Division being faced with both frontal and flank fire. Against these disadvantages, it is difficult with hindsight to envisage the success of such an attack.

The losses of the 4th Division including the Royal Warwicks attached from the 48th Division were 5,752. Three battalions suffered over 500 casualties, the 8/Royal Warwicks with 588, the 1/Hants 585 and the 1/E Lancs 502. The 4th Division had lost almost half its strength, a tragic loss of hardened soldiers fighting against impossible odds. There was little chance of replacing the losses with regular soldiers and the men of Kitchener's New Army would be called upon to fill the ranks. This they did and were soon to earn the respect of the surviving regulars of the 4th Division.

Objective 5

Beaumont Hamel, Y Ravine and Hawthorn Ridge

Battalions Engaged

Corps	Div.	Brig.	Bn.No.	Battalion
VIII	29	86	2	Royal Fusiliers
VIII	29	86	1	Lancs Fusiliers
VIII	29	86	16	Middlesex - Public Schools Battalion
VIII	29	86	1	Royal Dublin Fusiliers
VIII	29	87	2	South Wales Borderers
VIII	29	87	1	King's Own Scottish Borderers
VIII	29	87	1	Royal Inniskilling Fusiliers
VIII	29	87	1	Border
VIII	29	88	1	Essex
VIII	29	88	1	Newfoundland
VIII	29	88	4	Worcesters
VIII	29	88	2	Hampshires
VIII	29	0	2	Monmouths (pioneers)

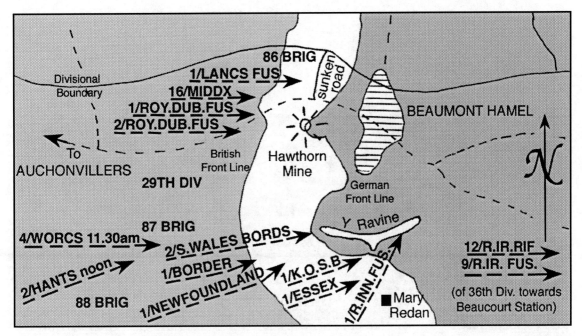

The area of attack of the 29th Division was Beaumont Hamel and the Hawthorn Ridge to the east. South of Beaumont Hamel was the German strongpoint called Y Ravine, named after its shape and cutting into the southern slope of Hawthorn Ridge. The whole of the 29th Division's dispositions was under direct German artillery observation - from the Schwaben Redoubt north of Thiepval, from the high ground behind Beaumont Hamel and from the Hawthorn Ridge.

The 86th Brigade on the extreme left of the division was to attack eastwards from north of Hawthorn Ridge. It was obvious that the Hawthorn Redoubt, having such a dominant view over the 86th Brigade, would present grave difficulties for any attack towards Beaumont Hamel. Accordingly, the 252nd Tunnelling Company was directed to mine the redoubt at the highest point. In under two months the miners had created a gallery of over 1,000 feet and a charge of 40,000 lbs. of ammonal was laid. The VIII Corps Commander, Lieut. General Sir A. G. Hunter-Weston had sought permission to detonate the mine around 3.00am in order that the redoubt could be taken and consolidated before the main attack at 7.30am. Permission was refused and it was finally agreed to explode the mine at 7.20am. There has been much criticism about this decision. It was obvious that if the mine were fired ten minutes before zero hour, the British artillery would have to lift its barrage to prevent the shelling of men in advanced positions. This would give the enemy ten minutes in which to mount their defences in complete safety and shell our forward, support and communication trenches. The Germans were quick to take advantage of these circumstances. It has been suggested that both Haig and Rawlinson thought the early firing of the mine on Hawthorn Ridge would draw German artillery from the south, particularly from Schwaben Redoubt and that this might be to the advantage of the all-important X Corps attack on Thiepval and the adjacent Schwaben Redoubt.

The Sunken Road, sometimes referred to as Hunter's Lane, just to the north of the Beaumont / Auchonvillers road and directly north of the Hawthorn Redoubt was about

White City   Redan Ridge   Argyll & Sutherland Highlanders Memorial   Sunken Road

1/LANCS. FUS.

16/MIDDX

The German view from the lip of the Hawthorne Mine Crater. The 1/Lancs Fus. advanced from left to right behind the 8th Argyle and Sutherland Memorial. The 16/Middx advanced across the sunken road where the Memorial now stands.

half way across No Man's Land. Today, an excellent view of Hunter's Lane can be enjoyed from the lip of the Hawthorn mine crater. A sunken road is one which has embankments on one or both sides and, therefore, gives protection to the infantry. It is like a ready-made trench. These were well-liked by the men but there was a disadvantage in that they could be easily identified and targeted by artillery fire by either side. Several attempts towards the end of June to take control of the Sunken Road by both sides had produced no positive result and so a tunnel was constructed by miners and the 2/Monmouth Pioneers prepared a trench from the end of the tunnel to Hunter's Lane. The tunnel was opened up in the early hours of the morning and B and D companies of the 1/Lancs Fusiliers assembled in the much contested Sunken Road at 3.00am on the 1st July.

Immediately after the firing of the Hawthorn Ridge mine, Stokes mortars opened fire on the German first line. Ten minutes later the infantry began its advance towards the first line of German defences. On leaving the Sunken Road the 1/Lancs Fusiliers were cut down by heavy machine gun fire and few men reached the German wire. Most were down in the first few yards after leaving the comparative safety of the Sunken Road. A and C companies had much difficulty in reaching the Sunken Road from their front line and lost heavily. The wounded were trying to get back to the front line and impaired the advance of the 16/Middlesex and the 1/Royal Dublin Fusiliers. They struggled up the communication trenches and by 8.00am were over the parapet. Uncut wire faced them and they stood no chance against the German defences and both battalions suffered heavy losses. As the whistles sounded throughout the line the leading formations of the 2/Royal Fusiliers dashed forward armed with machine guns and Stokes mortars to take possession of the newly formed crater. The Germans were already in possession and the Fusiliers were met with severe flanking and frontal fire. Prior to zero hour the Germans had only been using a selection of their artillery - now, they brought all their artillery resources into action and the whole of No Man's Land came under a very heavy barrage. The remainder of the Royal Fusiliers advanced towards Beaumont Hamel, their ultimate objective. Under heavy fire some veered to the crater where they managed to hold for a while. Those who succeeded in advancing to the German first line were killed.

The 87th Brigade was on the right of the attack and the 1/R. Inniskilling Fusiliers attacked down the slope towards Y Ravine. They continued under heavy fire and were held up by uncut wire. Some were able to pass through but not in sufficient numbers to make any gains. They were cut down and either killed or taken prisoner. The 2/S Wales Borderers on the left of the 87th Brigade advanced towards the left edge of Y Ravine but could not make any progress against the three machine guns facing them. In five minutes the leading companies were destroyed. The two support battalions, the 1/K.O.S.B. and the 1/Border fared no better and were raked by artillery and machine gun fire as they entered No Man's Land. Due to a misinterpretation of the pre-arranged flare signal, they should not have left the British front line. A German white artillery flare was mistaken for the British signal that the first German line had been reached. The British artillery continued its creeping barrage which did absolutely nothing to help the advancing infantry.

One of the major problems throughout the line was that of good communication. It appears that reports of soldiers advancing towards Beaumont Hamel had been exaggerated and Brig. General D. Caley decided to engage the two leading battalions of his 88th Brigade in an attack on the western end of Y Ravine. The 1/Newfoundland, known as the "Incomparables" from their exploits at Gallipoli, were to advance with the 1/Essex. The Essex could not get forward through the approach trenches - these were full of dead and wounded. The Newfoundlanders advanced in the open and immediately came under intense fire from Y Ravine. They fell in waves but still the rest continued. Many had fallen even before reaching the British wire and those who traversed the wire

The Caribou stands proud in Newfoundland Park on the site of the attack of the 29th Division. The park covers 80 acres and the trenches seen here are considered the best preserved in the Somme. Y Ravine is out of the picture, 500 meters north east of the Caribou

were cut down in No Man's Land. These hardy men from our island colony never faltered and their courage and determination may have been equalled elsewhere on the line but never surpassed. Every single officer was a casualty and the total loss of the Newfoundlanders was 710, the second highest casualty figure along the whole of the British front on the 1st July. Three companies of the 1/Essex managed with some difficulty to leave the trenches. Although showing the utmost determination only a few managed to reach the German first line where most were killed. The remainder, like those of the 1/Newfoundland lay dead or wounded in No Man's Land. The two remaining battalions of the 88th Brigade, the 4/Worcester and the 2/Hampshire were held back.

The total casualties of the 29th Regular Division was just over 5,000. Six battalions suffered over 500 casualties - the 1/Newfoundland 710, 2/Royal Fusiliers 561, 16/Middlesex 549, 1/ K.O.S.B. 552, 1/Inniskilling Fusiliers 568 and the 1/Border 575.

For the 29th Division, like the 4th, the heavy loss of so many experienced soldiers was a heavy price to pay for absolutely no gain. No other men could have done more - the German defences were just impenetrable. It was all over in an hour and a half and over four months were to pass before the Territorials of the 51st (Highland) Division captured Beaumont Hamel.

Objective 6
The Schwaben Redoubt,
St. Pierre Divion,
Beaucourt Station

Battalions Engaged

Corps	Div.	Brig.	Bn.No.	Battalion
X	36	107	8	Royal Irish Rifles (E. Belfast)
X	36	107	9	Royal Irish Rifles (W. Belfast)
X	36	107	10	Royal Irish Rifles (S. Belfast)
X	36	107	15	Royal Irish Rifles (N. Belfast)
X	36	108	11	Royal Irish Rifles (S. Antrim)
X	36	108	12	Royal Irish Rifles (Cen. Antrim)
X	36	108	13	Royal Irish Rifles (Co. Down)
X	36	108	9	Royal Irish Fusiliers (Co. Armagh, Monaghan & Cavan)
X	36	109	9	Royal Inniskilling Fusiliers (Co. Tyrone)
X	36	109	10	Royal Inniskilling Fusiliers (Co. Derry)
X	36	109	11	Royal Inniskilling Fusiliers - Donegal & Fermanagh
X	36	109	14	Royal Irish Rifles - Belfast Young Citizens
X	36	0	16	Royal Irish Rifles - 2nd Co. Down (pioneers)

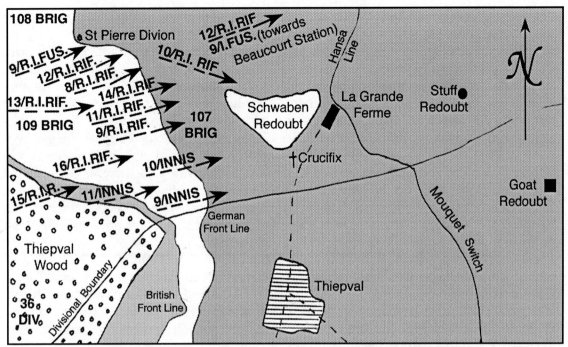

The Thiepval Ridge with its fortifications was considered to be the strongest of the German defences. The holder of the ridge had dominant views over a wide area. Some 900 meters to the north of the village lay the Schwaben Redoubt, a triangular shaped system of trenches and deep underground bunkers situated on the crest of Thiepval Spur. The area of the redoubt, often referred to as the "Parallelogram" by the Ulstermen, is to the immediate north east of Mill Road British Cemetery. Thiepval itself was in ruins but most of the houses had cellars and these were turned into good defensive positions having the advantage of being difficult to destroy. Amongst the heaps of rubble miniature redoubts were created. One and a half kilometers north west of Thiepval, the defences of St. Pierre Divion could provide both frontal and flank fire on any attack on the Schwaben Redoubt, Beaucourt or in the general direction of Beaumont Hamel or the Ancre valley. Stuff and Goat Redoubts presented further obstacles to the north east.

To the south east of Thiepval the ground descended gently to Mouquet Farm, another fortress and continued to Pozières. Two and a half kilometers to the south was the fortified village of Ovillers. To the south of Thiepval Memorial the Leipzig Redoubt would defend any attack on Thiepval from the south or the south west from Authuille. The Leipzig Salient or Granatloch, situated in a quarry, jutted out from the main redoubt and was a nest of machine guns. The Salient is easily recognisable today by the tall ring of trees which surrounds the quarry. Finally, the Wundt Werk and Nordwerk also protected Thiepval from the south.

These were the great obstacles facing the X Corps composed of the 36th (Ulster) Division which was to attack the Schwaben Redoubt, St. Pierre Divion and Beaucourt Station. The 32nd Division's task was the attack on Thiepval village, the Leipzig Salient and Mouquet Farm while the 49th (West Riding) Division was in reserve.

Objective Six concerns the attack by the Ulstermen of the 36th Division. All twelve battalions of the 107th, 108th and 109th Brigades were to be engaged as well as the divisional pioneers, the 16/Royal Irish Rifles. It is appropriate here to note the unusual formation of the 36th (Ulster) Division.

The political situation in Ireland in 1914 was delicate to say the least. The dominant Catholic population of the south wished to incorporate all Ireland into an independent state which was bitterly opposed by the mainly Protestant North. Feelings were running high during the Home Rule issue and there was much anti-British feeling at the time. In the north, Sir Edward Carson, leader of the Irish Unionists, aided by Sir James Craig (later Lord Craigavon, first Prime Minister of Northern Ireland) raised an illegal civil force of 80,000 men known familiarly as "Carson's Army" and elsewhere as the U.V.F. (Ulster Volunteer Force). It was raised to oppose any move by the Liberal Government to impose Home Rule on the Unionists. In the south, another illegal civilian force, the I.N.V. (Irish National Volunteers) had been formed to repulse any incursion into the south by the U.V.F. On the outbreak of war, both the I.N.V. and U.V.F., for obviously different political motives, volunteered their men, already armed and trained on military lines, to Lord Kitchener for service in his army, the former hoping the Home Rule Bill would be passed while the latter was pressing for a suspension of the Bill. Asquith assured Carson that the Home Rule Bill would be suspended until the end of hostilities. And so it was that the 36th (Ulster) Division was formed from the U.V.F. It is a fitting tribute to these Ulstermen that they were prepared to forget their political differences for the moment to answer the call to arms for King and Country.

The 108th and 109th brigades were assembled in Thiepval Wood where there was some semblance of safety, even though the wood had been shelled. The X Corps Commander, Lieut.-General Sir T. Morland and Major-General O.S.W. Nugent, the C.O. of the 36th Division were well aware of the difficulties facing them. In addition the men would have to attack uphill and mainly to the east facing the rising run. Thirty minutes before zero hour, trench mortar batteries opened fire on the German front line. Under cover of this fire the leading battalions of the 108th and 109th Brigades passed through the British pre-cut wire and crept to within a short distance of the German trenches.

At 7.30am precisely the buglers sounded the "advance" and the 9th and 10th Roy. Innis. Fus. of the 109th Brigade dashed forward under the cover of a good smoke screen. The enemy wire was well cut and the assault battalions stormed the first and then the support trenches before the Germans had time to realise what was happening. Pausing a moment to recuperate, they continued towards the enemy reserve line over 400 meters away. By this time the Germans had begun to organise themselves and the two battalions, particularly the 9/R. Innis. was badly hit. In spite of this, they continued their advance and entered not only the reserve trench but also the southern end of the Schwaben Redoubt. 400 prisoners were taken and sent back to the British lines. And still they advanced, arriving at the northern end of Mouquet Switch and the eastern face of the Schwaben Redoubt. Meanwhile, the 11/Royal Inniskilling Fus. and the 14/Royal Ir. Rifles debouched from Thiepval Wood to support the Inniskillings. By now the smoke screen had disappeared and the two battalions were caught by machine gun fire from the Crucifix, just north of Thiepval. Their dead and wounded lay thick in No Man's Land.

The 108th Brigade was on the extreme left and two battalions, the 12/Roy. Ir. Rifles and the 9/Roy. Ir. Fus. were to cross the Ancre and form the right hand battalions of the 29th Division to their immediate left. Their objective was Beaucourt Station and the area to the north. Men were falling before they reached their own wire and in front of them lay 600 meters of No Man's Land. The waves vanished under the withering fire from St. Pierre Divion and the Beaucourt Redoubt. The men went forward in small groups and sometimes, individually. Some men reached the enemy front line and here, those who survived continued towards Beaucourt Station where nearly all became casualties. The attack having failed, the German guns turned their fire to the south east and the 13th Rifles on the right of the River Ancre were hard hit. The survivors veered right towards the Hansa Line. The 11/Roy. Ir. Rifles, the right hand battalion of the 108th Brigade, supported by the 15/Roy. Ir. Rifles transferred to the 108th Brigade from the 107th, initially made good progress aided by the early smoke screen but were later caught by heavy machine gun fire and lost many men. The rest continued boldly and, having collected a few of the 13th Rifles, they continued under fire as far as Stuff Redoubt and the outskirts of Grandcourt.

At 7.30am the 107th brigade moved north from Aveluy Wood and leaving the swampy area of the Ancre, moved up through Thiepval Wood and awaited the order to advance. Due to the failure of the 32nd Division's attack on their right, the German machine guns in Thiepval turned their attention to Thiepval Wood and the wood was raked with constant fire causing many casualties. At 9.15am, three battalions, the 8th, 9th and 10th Royal Irish Rifles, left the wood. Many fell in No Man's Land but they passed through the gains of the 109th Brigade in Mouquet Switch and the Hansa Line taking some men with them from the 109th. Their objective, the Grandcourt Line, was 600 meters away and they caught up with the British barrage which caused heavy casualties. There can surely be nothing so disheartening than to be the victim of so called "friendly fire" They were obliged to lie in the summer grass with little cover until the creeping barrage was out of range. This delay gave the Germans time to man the line and they opened fire from Beaucourt Redoubt and Grandcourt causing heavy casualties. About fifty men were able to continue to Stuff Redoubt. Another group worked itself north in a trench towards Grandcourt. Some found shelter in a former gun emplacement in Battery Valley – the remainder had to wait it out under the German fire. Some were later to reach the German fourth Line. Out of bombs and ammunition they had to fall back to the 3rd Line.

The 16/Royal Irish Rifles (Pioneers) had moved up from Lancashire Dump towards St. Pierre Divion and tried to effect a trench through No Man's Land towards the German first line. Their casualties were so severe they had to abandon the work.

The Ulstermen had made a spectacular advance under terrible fire against the German positions. Surrounded by the enemy, almost out of ammunition and bombs, they clung desperately to their gains. It was all too clear that unless they could be supported to combat the inevitable German counter attacks, they could not hold. They had simply gone too far. It will be remembered that the 49th (West Riding) Division was in reserve and its C.O. Maj.-Gen. E.M. Perceval rushed to X Corps H.Q. and requested permission to put one of his brigades in immediate support of the 36th Division to consolidate the gains, but, after much discussion and delay, no positive decision was taken. It was nearly twelve hours after zero hour that the 146th Brigade of 49th Division was put at the disposal of the Ulstermen. It was too late - the Germans were now counter attacking in force with artillery and machine guns ranged in all directions. Two companies of 7/West Yorks of 146th Brigade went forward to support the gain on the edge of the Schwaben Redoubt but they veered left under fire and took some trenches between the redoubt and St. Pierre Divion. This did not help the Ulstermen who were, understandably disappointed. It has been recorded that the relationship between the 36th and 49th Divisions were somewhat strained afterwards. The position of the 36th Division was now desperate. Trainloads of German reinforcements were seen arriving in the direction of Grandcourt. The 16th Rifles pioneers were called forward with supplies of bombs, ammunition and water to the Schwaben Redoubt but the German barrage prevented them from getting their supplies up the line. As the light faded, the gallant 36th Division, victim of its own success, was ordered to return to the German first line which the 49th Division had occupied. Again, like the 4th Division to the north, the success of a divisional attack depended on the success of the flanking divisions. Here, the 36th Division had done all and more than was required of them but the failure of the 29th Division to the north west and the 32nd Division at Thiepval meant the gains could not be consolidated and exploited.

The losses of the 36th Division were 5,104. The men had fought with the utmost courage and determination. No less than four Victoria Crosses had been earned on that fateful day. The supreme medal was awarded to the following men: Captain E.N.F. Bell, 9/Royal Inniskilling Fusiliers, Lieutenant G.St.G.S. Cather, 9/Royal Irish Fusiliers, Private W.F. McFadzean, 14/Royal Irish Rifles, Private R. Quigg, 12/Royal Irish Rifles.

All battalions lost heavily, particularly the 13/Royal Irish Rifles with 595 casualties, 11/Royal Inniskilling Fusiliers 589 and the 9/Royal Irish Fusiliers 532. There can be no finer tribute to the Ulstermen than the famous words of Winston Churchill.

"Unconquerable, except by death, which they had conquered, they have set up a monument of native virtue which will command the wonder, the reverence and the gratitude of our island people so long as we endure as a nation of men".

The view facing the 108 and 109 Brigades of the 36th (Ulster) Division as they debouched from the northern edge of Thiepval Wood. The Ulster Tower can be seen in the centre, and the Schwaben Redoubt lies to the right. The Connaught Cemetery is in the foreground

Objective 7

Thiepval, the Leipzig Salient, Mouquet Farm

Battalions Engaged

Corps	Div.	Brig.	Bn.No.	Battalion
X	32	14	19	Lancs Fusiliers - 3rd Salford Pals
X	32	14	1	Dorsets
X	32	14	2	Manchesters
X	32	14	15	Highland Light Infantry - Glasgow Tramways
X	32	96	16	Northumberland Fusiliers - Newcastle Commercials
X	32	96	2	Royal Inniskilling Fusiliers
X	32	96	15	Lancs Fusiliers - 1st Salford Pals
X	32	96	16	Lancs Fusiliers - 2nd Salford Pals
X	32	97	11	Border, The Lonsdales
X	32	97	2	King's Own Yorkshire Light Infantry
X	32	97	16	Highland Light Infantry - Glasgow Boys Brigade
X	32	97	17	Highland Light Infantry - Glasgow Commercials
X	32	0	17	Northumberland Fusiliers - Newcastle Railway Pals (pioneers)

The Thiepval Memorial to the Missing on the Somme where 73,000 names are recorded. Standing on the high ground of Thiepval Ridge on part of the site of the ruins of Thiepval Château, the Memorial is visible from many parts of the battlefield. Designed by Sir Edwin Lutyens, it was inaugurated by the Prince of Wales in 1932.

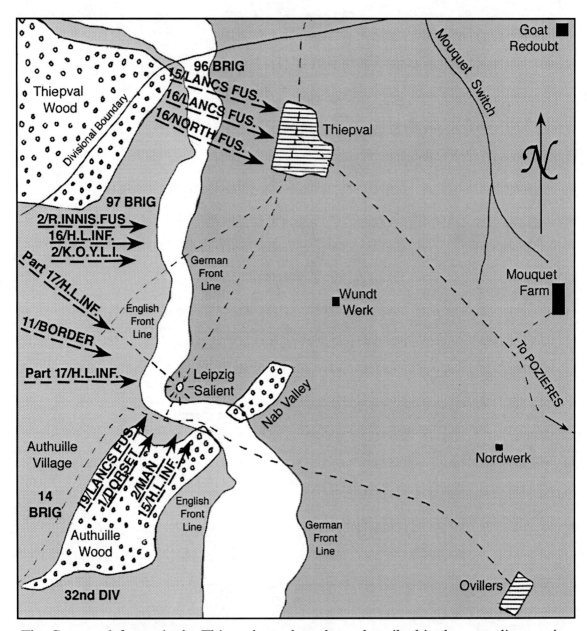

The German defences in the Thiepval area have been described in the preceding section in the account of the 36th (Ulster) Division attack on the Schwaben Redoubt. Of these defences, those in Thiepval, the Wundt Werk and Nord Werk were to prove serious obstacles to the 32nd Division whose objectives were those stated above. The 96th and 97th Brigades were assembled on the western slopes of Thiepval Spur and the plan was to attack the spur from the Leipzig Salient to Thiepval. The 14th Brigade was in reserve. The assembly trenches had been laboriously dug at the end of June in preparation for the attack. The ground around Thiepval and Authuille is of a chalky substance but with flintstone boulders making excavation very tiring for the men involved.

The daunting task facing the 96th Brigade was the capture of Thiepval. The leading battalions, the 15th and 16th Lancs. Fus. (1st and 2nd Salford Pals) were destined to fall in horrendous numbers before the intense machine gun fire from the ruined houses and Thiepval Fort. The German defences facing them were of the highest quality. There was some hand to hand fighting at the wire but most never reached this obstacle, they were cut down in waves as soon as they left the trenches. In spite of the losses, a few men were seen to enter the village and it was wrongly assumed that at least a part of Thiepval was being held by the Lancs. Fus. For this reason, Thiepval was not shelled during the day and the German gunners were left unmolested. A and B companies of the 16/Northumberland Fus. along with two companies of the 2/Royal Inniskilling Fusiliers, moved forward in support, but were met with a hail of bullets. The Germans were so confident they were on the parapet to achieve a better aim. C company of the Northumberland Fus. now moved forward in support but these unfortunate men fared no better. D Company prepared to advance but when the leading platoon fell before the fire, the rest of the men were mercifully held back. The remaining two companies of the 2/Royal Inniskilling Fus. which had been in reserve in the Ancre valley, were ordered forward at 9.15am from Johnson Post at the east of Thiepval Wood to make contact with the 15/Lancs. Fus. who were (supposedly) in Thiepval village. They were hit by fire from Thiepval Fort and had to take cover. Several subsequent attempts to cross No Man's Land were doomed to failure and the attack had to be called off.

The 97th Brigade was assembled on a frontage of 800 meters and the 16/H.L.I. (Glasgow Boy's Brigade) and the 17/H.L.I. (Glasgow Commercials) along with the 2/K.O.Y.L.I. were to take the Leipzig Salient and then the 11/Border was to follow through clearing the trenches as it advanced to join the other battalions in the Leipzig Salient whereafter the whole brigade was to advance on Mouquet Farm. Prior to zero hour Stokes mortars had laid a heavy barrage on the first German trenches and at 7.23am the Highlanders crept forward to occupy forward positions within 30 meters of the enemy trenches. Seven minutes later the barrage lifted and with the wire well cut, the 17/H.L.I. on the right dashed forward and were in the tip of the Leipzig Salient before the Germans had time to react. Some prisoners were taken back to the British Lines. The leading companies continued their advance towards the Hindenberg Trench - the route to the Wundt Werk, but heavy fire from the latter stopped the advance. Brig. General Jardine, C.O. of the 97th Brigade ordered part of the artillery to be redirected to the German defences beyond the Leipzig Salient and on the Wundt Werk; this in contradiction to the strict orders regarding the creeping artillery barrage. Although against higher orders, this was a wise decision, it being obvious the Highlanders were completely pinned down with no possible chance of continuing towards their objective. Thus, the survivors were able to retire to the Leipzig Salient. The companies of the 2/K.O.Y.L.I. were now moving up in close support and entered the salient and assisted in the consolidation of the gain. Subsequent attempts to cross the open ground towards the Wundt Werk failed as did the attempts to bomb along the German trenches beyond the salient.

Sixty minutes after zero hour the 11/Border moved forward in support. With the smoke and haze of the battle, they could not see or know the progress of the other three battalions. Theirs was supposedly a clearing up operation and subsequently an advance with the remainder of the Brigade towards Mouquet Farm. The Borders came under the most severe enfilade fire from the Nord Werk causing heavy casualties to the right companies. A few small groups on the left succeeded in reaching the Leipzig Salient which offered some protection. The 16/H.L.I. on the left of its sister battalion and supported by the two remaining companies of the 2/K.O.Y.L.I. found the German wire only partially cut. In spite of the heavy Stokes mortar barrage some Germans were firing from the ruined château and houses even as the men were creeping towards their forward positions. At zero hour they dashed forward to find the few gaps in the wire were covered by machine gun fire and many met their death against the wire. The left and centre could not move at all and they lay in No Man's Land, pinned down for the whole day. A few small groups on the right managed to join the Borders and reach the Leipzig Salient. The Wundt Werk, their objective remained inviolate. The battalion losses were over 500 officers and men.

At 7.00am the reserve Brigade, the 14th, moved from Authuille to its designated positions in Authuille Wood. The 1/Dorset and the 19/Lancs. Fus. (3rd Salford Pals) were immediately swept by machine gun fire, the Germans guessing correctly that support battalions would be moving up through the wood. They suffered heavy casualties and the Dorsets had difficulty in advancing over the bodies of their comrades. The situation worsened for the two leading companies as they debouched from the wood over the open ground. Fire from the Nord Werk reduced their numbers even further. Less than seventy men managed to reach the comparative safety of Leipzig Salient. The other two companies of the Dorsets could not get forward and were obliged to remain in the wood.

The Lancashire Fusiliers followed and, in spite of a smoke screen, their fate was sealed and three quarters of the men were down. Only forty men succeeded in reaching the salient. It was extremely difficult to get accurate information to divisional headquarters, practically all the cables had been destroyed by the German artillery. The only means was to send runners. This was very dangerous for the men chosen for this task and often, two and sometimes three runners were sent with the same message. They were targeted by snipers and many runners perished in their attempts to get vital information through to H.Q. It is assumed this lack of communication was the cause of the divisional C.O. Major General W.H. Rycroft to state that the 19/Lancs. Fus. did not appear to have left their trenches. Fortunately, the Fusiliers were not aware of this statement - it is just as well - they had lost about 75% of their attacking force. When the results of the 14th Brigades supporting action were at last known by H.Q., Rycroft decided to hold back the 15/H.L.I. (Glasgow Tramways) and the 2/Manchester for the time being.

However, at 1.45pm two companies of the 2/Manchester approached the salient well to the left to avoid fire from the Nordwerk. The remaining Manchesters joined them in the early evening. They found a mixture of Highlanders, Borders, K.O.Y.L.I., Lancs. Fus. and Dorsets in rather a confused state. Dead and wounded were everywhere. The men had been subjected to artillery and machine gun fire throughout the whole day. In spite of this they repelled counter attacks by German bombers approaching via their own trenches. During one such attack, Sgt. J.Y. Turnbull of the 17/H.L.I. was to be posthumously awarded the Victoria Cross for his action in defending the salient. Later in the evening two Russian saps were prepared which would offer safe communication for troops and supplies.

Hundreds upon hundreds of wounded lay near the wire and in No Man's Land not daring to move for fear of being shot by one of the many German snipers. They had to wait until nightfall to try to make their way back to the British front line. The casualties

The 97 Brigade of the 32nd Division attacked the Leipzig Salient, a quarry, now overgrown with trees. Here, Sgt. Turnbull earned his posthumous Victoria Cross and is buried in the Lonsdale Cemetery, the walls of which can be seen on the extreme left of the picture.

of the 32nd Division were 3,949 officers and other ranks. The few Lancashire Fusiliers who had been observed entering Thiepval were not seen again and the village remained totally in German hands. The capture of the Leipzig Salient was to be the only gain of the day in the sector. It was a gain of considerable importance but one which could not be exploited until the fall of Thiepval and the silencing of the two strongpoints, the Nord Werk and the Wundt Werk.

Heroic efforts had been vainly made to penetrate the German defences and it has been said that only bullet-proof soldiers could have taken Thiepval. The Wundt Werk was not taken until the 14th September and Thiepval finally fell to the 18th Division on the 26th September.

On the 26th November, eight days after the Somme campaign had ground to a halt in the mud, the 16/H.L.I., the Glasgow Boy's Brigade, were on their own fighting for their lives in Frankfurt Trench just four kilometers to the north west of Thiepval. These men, out of ammunition and food, nearly all wounded, surrounded by their dead friends and fighting with their last weapon, the bayonet, were finally overwhelmed by the Germans. The few who had survived the horror of the first day of the battle and further engagements over the next four and half months could now claim to have fought its very last action.

Objective 8

Ovillers

Battalions Engaged

Corps	Div.	Brig.	Bn.No.	Battalion
III	8	23	2	Devons
III	8	23	2	Middlesex
III	8	23	2	West Yorks
III	8	23	2	Scottish Rifles
III	8	25	2	Lincolns
III	8	25	2	Royal Berks
III	8	25	1	Royal Irish Rifles
III	8	25	2	Rifle Brigade
III	8	70	11	Sherwood Foresters - attached to 8th Div. from 23rd
III	8	70	8	King's Own Yorkshire - attached to 8th Div. from 23rd
III	8	70	8	Yorks and Lancs - attached to 8th Div. from 23rd
III	8	70	9	Yorks and Lancs - attached to 8th Div. from 23rd
III	8	0	22	Durham Light Infantry (Pioneers)

The daunting stretch of open ground facing the three Brigades of the 8th Division during their attack on Ovillers. Advancing with literally no cover, they were cut down by machine gun fire from the well-entrenched German defences.

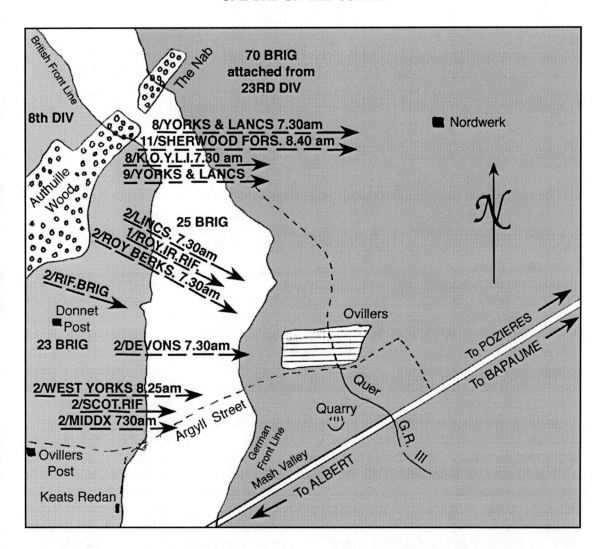

It will be seen on the map that Ovillers-la-Boisselle, referred to simply as Ovillers, is situated just north of the Albert-Bapaume road, south-east of Authuille Wood and two kilometers west-south-west of Pozières. The 8th Division, composed of the 70th Brigade on the left, the 25th in the centre and the 23rd on the right was to attack Ovillers and the rising ground north of the village known as Ovillers Spur. It was a difficult task facing the division and success depended to a large extent on the advances of the flanking divisions - the 32nd to the north at Thiepval and the 34th to the south at La Boisselle.

The two leading battalions of the 70th Brigade were the 8th York & Lancs, ex miners from the Rotherham district and the 8th K.O.Y.L.I. They were soldiers of the New Army and this was to be their baptism of fire. They commenced their attack at 7.30am and at first, they made some progress but as they approached the German trenches to the west of the Nordwerk and the Nordwerk itself they came under heavy fire from this position and from Leipzig Redoubt to the north. The week-long barrage had not destroyed these defences and the men fell in waves. The attack of the 32nd Division on Thiepval and the Leipzig Redoubt had failed apart from a small lodgement in the Leipzig Salient and this confirmed the worst fears of the 8th Division's C.O. who had, in fact, made a request to retard the attack of the 70th Brigade but this was refused by General Rawlinson. The initial advance had now lost its impetus and the 9th York & Lancs were ordered to move forward to support the failing attack but were cut down by machine gun fire from Thiepval Spur and in a few minutes, half the men were casualties. The last of the four battalions, the 11th Sherwood Foresters went forward in two waves, striding over the corpses of their fallen comrades and few reached the German wire. Those who struggled to traverse the wire were easy targets for the German machine gunners. By now the Germans were organising a counter attack to drive out the few men who still clung to the gains west of the Nordwerk and by evening the whole area was back in German hands. These men of the New Army had come through their baptism of fire with great courage and determination. The four battalion commanders were casualties and the Official History records that the casualties of the 70th Brigade were 1996 officers and other ranks.

The men of the 25th Brigade were regular soldiers and had seen action at Neuve Chappelle and elsewhere and it was considered their attack on Ovillers would have a reasonable chance of success as the infantry could not be seen by the defenders until the last four hundred yards of their attack. At 7.30am the 2nd Lincs and the 2nd Royal Berks left the trenches. Within twenty minutes the Lincolns had reached the German front line and a few managed to reach the German second line but these gallant men were driven out by consistent enfilade fire. No Man's Land was devastated by German artillery and although the shell holes provided temporary cover for wounded men, any support for the Lincolns was impossible. The Berkshires were cut down from intense fire from rifle and machine guns concealed in the ruins of the village and were unable to make any significant advance. The 2nd Royal Irish Rifles went forward in support but had already suffered heavy casualties from the German barrage before leaving the British front line trench. They made a supreme effort to cross No Man's Land but their fate under the intense barrage was sealed and the Rifles' losses were in excess of 450, only ten men managed to cross to support their comrades. It was now obvious that a successful attack on Ovillers could not be undertaken until the German defences on the Thiepval Spur had been neutralised.

The 23rd Brigade on the right, regular soldiers like their comrades of the 25th, were to attack from the south west of Ovillers through Mash Valley with a daunting width of No Man's Land facing them. The two leading battalions, the 2nd Devons and the 2nd Middlesex commenced their attack with the other brigades at 7.30am. In spite of heavy fire from the defenders of Ovillers and the German R110 Regiment north east of La Boisselle, a few men passed through the German front line trench and, amazingly, some advanced a further two hundred yards to the German second line but here, any further advance was impossible under the intense enfilade fire. A mere handful of men reached the Albert-Bapaume road but, as far as is known, there were no survivors. Lieut.-Col. Sandys, the C.O. of the 2nd Middlesex had voiced his fears of his men being held up at the uncut wire but his views were not well received by his superiors. No Man's Land was some 750 yards wide where his battalion had to cross and his fears became an obsession. He was a gallant officer and respected by his men. He was wounded in the attack and had to be withdrawn to the rear and was later transferred to England to recover from his wounds. In the evening of the 1st July only one officer and twenty eight men answered the roll call. On hearing the fate of his men, he became so depressed that he shot himself in his hotel room in London and died a few days later. At 8.25am the 2nd West Yorks moved forward in support losing over 250 men in the British front line trench through artillery fire and their total losses in trying to cross No Man's Land amounted to 430 officers and men. Very few were able to support the Devons and Middlesex battalions. The advance of the 34th Division to the right of the 23rd Brigade had failed and the German guns were able to execute their deadly work on the attackers at Mash Valley. The 2nd Scottish Rifles were about to commence their advance but thankfully, the order was cancelled and this battalion at least, was spared.

All three brigades had displayed the utmost courage and discipline but they could claim no permanent gains. The Official History records that the total casualties for the 8th Division were 5,121 officers and men.

From Gommecourt in the north down through Serre, Beaumont-Hamel, the Schwaben Redoubt, Thiepval and now at Ovillers, the attacks had failed. The 36th (Ulster) Division at the Schwaben Redoubt had advanced further than any other but could not be reinforced and had to retire. One bitter lesson was learned on that terrible day - unprotected infantry cannot successfully advance, particularly uphill and in daylight, against enemy fortifications with well-placed guns and artillery.

Objective 9
La Boisselle

Battalions Engaged

Corps	Div.	Brig.	Bn.No.	Battalion
III	34	101	15	Royal Scots - 1st Edinburgh City
III	34	101	16	Royal Scots - 2nd Edinburgh City
III	34	101	10	Lincolns - Grimsby Chums
III	34	101	11	Suffolks - Cambridge
III	34	102	20	Northumberland Fusiliers - 1st Tyneside Scottish
III	34	102	21	Northumberland Fusiliers - 2nd Tyneside Scottish
III	34	102	22	Northumberland Fusiliers - 3rd Tyneside Scottish
III	34	102	23	Northumberland Fusiliers - 4th Tyneside Scottish
III	34	103	24	Northumberland Fusiliers - 1st Tyneside Irish
III	34	103	25	Northumberland Fusiliers - 2nd Tyneside Irish
III	34	103	26	Northumberland Fusiliers - 3rd Tyneside Irish
III	34	103	27	Northumberland Fusiliers - 4th Tyneside Irish
III	34	0	18	Northumberland Fusiliers (pioneers)

Note: N.F. = Northumberland Fusiliers

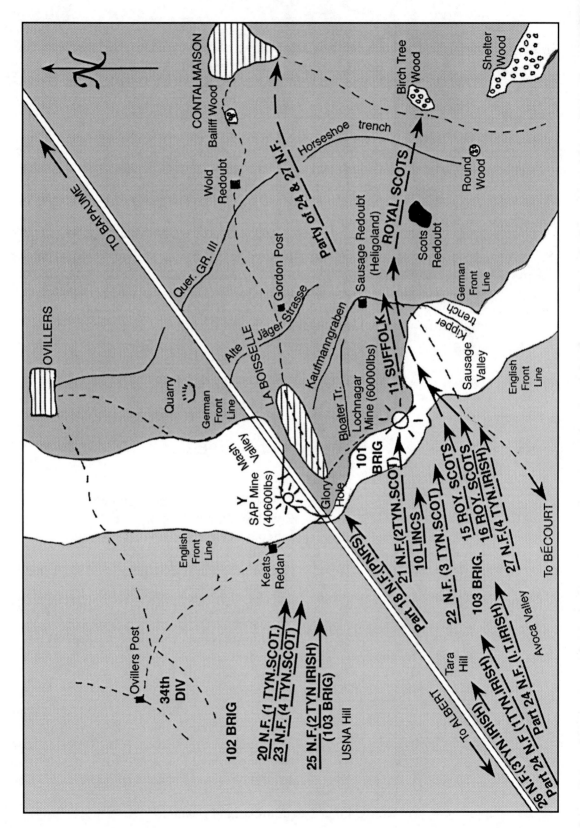

The village of La Boisselle lies on the main Albert/Bapaume road and the fall of the village would mean the opening of the way to Bapaume through Pozières and an entry on to the Fricourt Spur towards Contalmaison. The German fortifications were, therefore, designed to protect this important position, their front line reaching the village from the south east, passing just to the south of it and then turning sharp right and running along the main road before heading north to the west of Ovillers. The village itself was also well fortified, with Sausage Redoubt, Schwaben Höhe and Scots Redoubt to the south east. A thousand meters to the north, the defences of Ovillers would pour flank fire in any attack towards Pozières from the north side of the main road up Mash Valley.

From the fact that La Boisselle lay in a shallow valley, both British and German had dominant views of the battle area and both sides could easily identify the trenches from the white chalk spoil heaps. However, the advantage was on the German side as once the attackers reached the village the ground began to rise.

In face of these obstacles, the 179th Tunnelling Company laid two mines, Y Sap, a few yards north of the main road opposite the south western tip of La Boisselle with a charge of 40,600 lbs. of ammonal and the second called Lochnagar with a total charge of 60,000 lbs. on the German position Schwaben Höhe. This second mine had two charges of 36,000 and 24,000 lbs., some 60 feet distant at a depth of 52 feet. The excavation of the underground galleries was painfully slow work, executed with the point of a bayonet for noise reduction purposes. Every endeavour was made to prevent boulders from falling to the floor and progress was around 18 inches in 24 hours. It was decided to fire the mines two minutes before zero hour hoping the explosions would destroy the strongpoints and that the ensuing lips would provide protection from flank fire.

The 34th Division under the command of Major-General E.C. Ingouville-Williams was designated to attack these defences. The division's three brigades were the 101st, 102nd and 103rd, the first being a mixture of English and Scottish battalions and the second and third being the Tyneside Scottish and Tyneside Irish respectively. The divisional pioneers were the 18/N.F. All thirteen battalions were to be engaged on the 1st July.

On the night of June 30th British patrols sent forward to clear a way through the wire found the Germans very active. It was obvious the long barrage had not achieved the desired result. A Stokes mortar barrage was laid on the village and a forward emplacement prepared in No Man's Land to bomb Sausage Redoubt. The Germans soon had the range and the mortar battery which had been doing good work ceased when all the bombers were either killed or wounded.

The width of No Man's Land varied considerably, from 45 meters at the Glory Hole to a maximum of about 730 meters elsewhere. The plan was not to attack La Boisselle directly but pass on either flank, bombing parties being sent to clear the village from both flanks.

The 101st Brigade was assembled adjacent to Chapes Spur which is north of Bécourt Wood. The left assault battalion was the 10/Lincoln (Grimsby Chums) with the 11/Suffolk (Cambridge) in immediate support. They were ordered to wait five minutes after the firing of the Lochnagar mine to avoid injury from falling debris. It is now known that the debris from any explosion of this nature only takes a very short time to settle and the Lincolns and Suffolks delay was to prove very costly. At 7.28am the two mines were fired. The 60,000 lbs. of ammonal at Lochnagar created a great burst of flame and debris and the shock waves were such that some soldiers in trenches 250 meters distant suffered

At 7.28am on the 1st July 60,000 pounds of Ammonal were exploded and made the Lochnagar Crater, south of La Boisselle. The crater has remained dry in this sector of the Front Line, whereas only six kilometers to the northeast at High Wood a small crater quickly filled with water and became a pond.

leg fractures. The unsuspecting Germans of the 110th Regiment on the Schwaben Höhe were literally blown to pieces. The Lincolns and Suffolks advanced past the south eastern tip of the crater towards Bloater Trench and came under intense fire from Sausage Redoubt (Heligoland) and both battalions lost heavily. A few Lincolns managed to reach the eastern lip of the crater, giving some protection, at least, for the time being. The supporting Suffolks fought desperately to enter Sausage Redoubt and, on arriving at the parapet, were exterminated by flame-throwers.

In the early hours of 30th June, the right assault battalion the 15/Royal Scots had moved to advanced positions some two thirds of the distance across No Man's Land. They crossed the remaining 200 meters under fire from Sausage Redoubt on the left and also from Bloater Trench and the attack ground to a halt. Two attempts to reinforce them by the pioneer battalion and the Royal Engineers failed. The Scots took breath, picked themselves up and continued with the 16/Royal Scots close behind. The fire was so intense that both the Royal Scots were forced away from their objectives, Sausage and Scots Redoubts and veered to the east and eventually reached the Fricourt/Contalmaison road close to Birch Tree Wood. Here, they met up with contingents of the 21st Division of the XV Corps. It was essential they reorganised and the 15/Royal Scots moved towards Peake Wood, the 16/Royal Scots remaining in support near Round Wood. They were surrounded with Germans in front, at La Boisselle on the left rear and in the rear from the German trenches. In spite of their desperate situation, they, along with a few men from the 27/N.F. and Suffolks, attacked and seized Scots Redoubt. This improved the situation although Sausage Redoubt was still untaken. In spite of a combined attack later in the day by contingents of the 34th and 21st Divisions, this stronghold which had caused such terrible losses remained untaken. Strong German counter attacks forced the 15/Royal Scots to retire to Shelter Wood. The failure of the Royal Scots to take Sausage Redoubt, although all will concede it was a most difficult task, was largely responsible for the terrible losses of the Lincolns and Suffolks, the former losing 477 officers and men and the latter over five hundred (see details at end of this section).

British observers, having seen that Sausage Redoubt was still in enemy hands, ordered the 24/N.F. of the 103rd Brigade to halt their advance. Unfortunately, the order was received too late and the Fusiliers along with the other three battalions of the Tyneside Irish, were already on their way down the long slope towards the British front line trenches, approximately a thousand meters away. They presented a perfect target for the German gunners and within ten minutes the bulk of the gallant Tyneside Irish had perished on the slopes. A few, mainly mixed 24th and 27th Fusiliers, sheltered by some natural geographical feature continued, following at the start the path of the Royal Scots but later keeping north of Scots Redoubt and advanced to the very outskirts of Contalmaison. Parties of these two battalions helped in the taking of Scots Redoubt and others in the defence of Shelter Wood with the 15/Royal Scots.

The remaining battalion of the 103rd Brigade, the 25/N.F. also suffered heavily on its downhill approach to the north of the main road where they formed the rear of the left column of the 102nd Brigade.

The Glory Hole at La Boisselle was held by part of the 18/N.F (Pioneers). The cratered ground - where death and glory were found on that fateful day - is still visible some eighty years later.

The attractive Contalmaison Château remained in the hands of the Hangest/Mousquet family from the 16th to the end of the 18 century when the seigneury later passed to the Debray/Peyrou family. During the great War it was occupied by German troops until the château became the target of the Allied artillery.

By the end of the battle of the Somme there was nothing left of this distinctive building but a low pile of dust and rubble - there was nothing left to re-build.

The Tyneside Scots of the 102nd Brigade were situated north and south of the main Bapaume Road. The 20th and 23rd N.F. were to the north supported by the 25/N.F. from 103rd Brigade as mentioned above. The British bombardment had not silenced the German defences in and around the village and as soon as the men left the trenches at the start of Mash Valley with some 700 meters of open ground in front of them, they were cut down in hundreds. They could take no shelter and advanced with great courage until they fell. What a sad but magnificent sight it must have been - each company being played into battle by its piper who continued to play his stirring music until he fell.

The remaining two battalions, the 21st and 22nd N.F. supported by the survivors of the 26th N. Fusiliers were south of the main road. Here, No Man's Land was not wide and immediately upon the firing of the two mines they leaped forward and were in the first German trenches. Hereafter, the lines thinned under the withering fire but the survivors passed over the Kaufmann Graben and the Alte Jäger Strasse. The advance had now lost its momentum and although a few men reached Bailiff Wood on the outskirts of Contalmaison, the remainder were pushed back by the enemy and eventually retired to Kaufmann Graben where they consolidated.

Filling the gap between the left and right elements of 102nd Brigade, C Company of the 18/N.F. pioneers held the sector around the Glory Hole.

Ingouville-Williams had committed all his brigades and most of the pioneers. He had, therefore, no reserves to send forward. Corps H.Q. put the 9/Welsh of the 19th Division in reserve at his disposal but the order to attack was later cancelled, the decision having been taken for the 19th Division to attack La Boisselle after sunset. The only real gains of the day were the capture of Scots Redoubt and the German forward trenches. The left wing of the attack had failed with horrendous casualties. The centre and right wing battalions were very hard hit but the advance of a party of 24th and 27th N.F. resembles the magnificent advance of the 36th (Ulster) further to the north.

Here, as the Ulstermen at the Schwaben Redoubt, the few Tyneside Irish were too few in number to exploit their distance gains.

At least, here at La Boisselle, there was a foothold in the German defence system - the first success in the long line of failed attacks south from Gommecourt to Ovillers, apart from a hold in the Leipzig Redoubt by the 32nd Division which did not result in the capture of Thiepval. The taking of Scots Redoubt by the 34th Division was of great assistance to the 19th (Western) Division which took La Boisselle on the 4th July after three days of bitter fighting.

As the British front line wound its way from La Boisselle firstly south east towards Fricourt and Mametz and then east to Montauban the divisions of the XV and XIII Corps were to enjoy an increasing measure of success.

The total casualties of the 34th Division were the highest of all the divisions engaged on that fateful day - a staggering 6,380 officers and men. All the thirteen battalions suffered very heavily, particularly the following:

23/N.F. (4th Tyneside Scottish)	629
24/N.F. (1st Tyneside Irish)	620
20/N.F. (1st Tyneside Scottish)	584
27/N.F. (4th Tyneside Irish)	539
22/N.F. (3rd Tyneside Scottish)	537
11/Suffolk (Cambridge)	527
15/Royal Scots (1st Edinburgh City)	513

The scars of this epic struggle can still be seen today. The lip of great Lochnagar crater can be seen on the right of the Bapaume road from Albert and access is signposted in the village. It is now privately owned, purchased by Mr. Richard Dunning to prevent it from being filled in and to preserve it for all time. It is an impressive sight. The cratered ground of the Glory Hole gives some idea of the severity of the bombardment. On the main road at the entry to La Boisselle from Albert is the Tyneside Memorial Seat while in the village, near the church are memorials to the 34th and 19th (Western) Divisions.

Objective 10

The Attack from the South West of Contalmaison

Battalions Engaged

Corps	Div.	Brig.	Bn.No.	Battalion
XV	21	62	12	Northumberland Fusiliers
XV	21	62	13	Northumberland Fusiliers
XV	21	62	1	Lincolns
XV	21	62	10	Green Howards
XV	21	63	8	Lincolns
XV	21	63	8	Somerset Light Infantry
XV	21	63	4	Middlesex
XV	21	63	10	Yorks and Lancs
XV	21	64	9	King's Own Yorkshire Light Infantry
XV	21	64	10	King's Own Yorkshire Light Infantry
XV	21	64	1	East Yorks
XV	21	64	15	Durham Light Infantry
XV	21	0	14	Northumberland Fusiliers (pioneers)

Objective 11

The Attack on Fricourt Village by the 50th Brigade attached to 21st Division from 17th (Northern) Division

Battalions Engaged

Corps	Div.	Brig.	Bn.No.	Battalion
XV	17	50	10	West Yorks
XV	17	50	7	East Yorks
XV	17	50	7	Green Howards
XV	17	50	6	Dorsets
XV	17	0	7	Yorks and Lancs (pioneers)

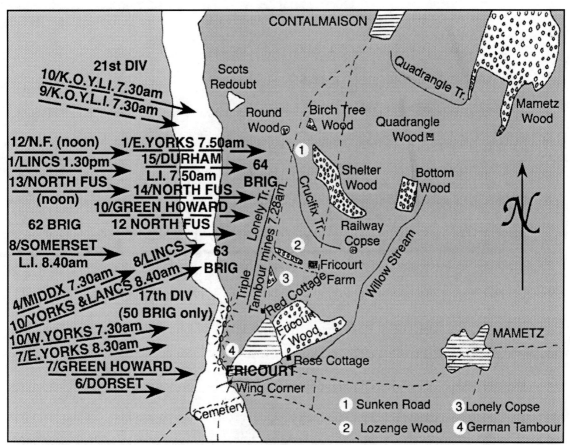

The 21st Division was assembled west of the Fricourt to Contalmaison road at points between Fricourt and Round Wood. It faced a strong German defence system including Fricourt Farm, Crucifix and Lonely Trenches and the Sunken Road. The triangular shape of Fricourt Wood offered excellent defensive positions. Fricourt itself was well fortified with very deep dugouts, some having two storeys, capable of withstanding the British bombardment. No Man's Land varied between 200 and 300 meters.

It was decided not to attack the strong defences of Fricourt directly but to isolate it by flanking attacks by the 21st Division on the left and the 7th Division on the right. The 50th Brigade (attached from 17th Division) was to assault the village later in the day.

The 64th Brigade was on the left wing and in touch with the 34th Division on its left. The two assault battalions, the 9th and 10th K.O.Y.L.I. moved to forward positions helped by a prepared Russian sap but even before the British bombardment reached its conclusion, the German machine guns had been brought into action and swept the whole of No Man's Land. At 7.30am the Yorkshiremen went forward from hole to hole still under heavy fire but they stuck to their task and, finding the wire well cut, stormed the enemy front line trench, with the rear companies following close behind. The support battalions, the 1/East Yorks on the left and the 15/D.L.I. on the right moved forward. The enemy fire had not diminished and both support battalions were reduced to almost half strength. The thinned numbers joined the Yorkshiremen. After a brief pause the remnants of all four battalions moved forward once more and seized the support trench. Two lines of trenches and about 200 prisoners had been taken in ten minutes, but it had been a

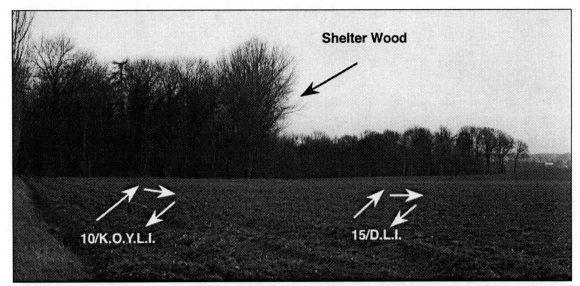

Shelter Wood

10/K.O.Y.L.I.

15/D.L.I.

Shelter Wood, which at first withstood the attack of the 10/K.O.Y.L.I and the 15/D.L.I., but was taken the next day by their own 21 Division.

costly affair. They were now well forward and had to wait for the creeping barrage to move forward before attempting to cross the considerable width of ground between themselves and the Sunken Road. Enemy fire was still pouring from Shelter and Birch Tree Woods and Fricourt Farm and the men moved forward again from hole to hole suppressing isolated pockets of German resistance with either bomb or bayonet. In 30 minutes they had covered 1,500 meters of open ground and were now in the Sunken Road leading from Fricourt to Contalmaison. Here the men halted to consolidate the defences in the Sunken Road and Lonely Trench, just to the west. However, parties from the four battalions went forward and occupied the northern end of Crucifix Trench. The immediate concern was to consolidate the entry as the creeping barrage would soon pass over the German strongpoints and a counter attack was almost inevitable. With very little

cover, yet more men fell while trying to strengthen this position. Fortunately, the British artillery was able, for the time being, to keep most of the German infantry at a distance. Some of the 1/East Yorks moved up from the Sunken Road to Crucifix Trench where they found some Royal Scots from the 34th

Monsieur Bernard Maes, a Fricourt farmer, clearing the foundations of the original Fricourt Farm where the ground remained fallow for sixty-five years. M. Maes has been cultivating the land for the past fifteen years and removes a various number of cart-loads of rubble each year.

The Ferme du Bois was built after 1918 some 150 meters west of the original Fricourt Farm which was completely destroyed by the British artillery.

Division under attack. The Scots and Yorkshiremen repulsed the attack driving the enemy back into Shelter Wood. The 64th Brigade was now well ahead of units on either flank and received orders to halt their advance. The 1/Lincoln and 10/Green Howard, both from the 62nd brigade, moved up to strengthen the weakened flanks, the Lincolns to the left of the 64th Brigade to fill the gap where the 101st Brigade of the 34th Division should have been, and the Green Howards to the right of the 63rd Brigade.

The 12th and 13th N.F. of 62nd Brigade were sent forward in the early evening to relieve the exhausted 64th Brigade which had taken all its objectives and this was completed about dawn on the following day.

The 63rd Brigade on the right of the 64th, was to take Fricourt Farm. A very heavy Stokes mortar bombardment commenced at 7.22am and four minutes later a smoke screen was laid. At 7.28am the triple Tambour mines were fired. (25,000 lbs., 15,000 lbs. and 9,000 lbs.) under the German line known as The Tambour. The mines were a diversion to distract enemy flank fire from the German Tambour strongpoint, just south of the triple explosion. The British mortar fire had not silenced the enemy machine guns and the two leading companies of the 4/Middx. suffered so heavily while creeping forward to their advanced positions in No Man's Land that they had to return to their trench. They rested only briefly and were out of the trench again before zero hour when the same fire reduced their ranks again. Small groups formed as the survivors struggled on towards the centre section of the Sunken Road. The rear companies of the Middlesex were to face the same fire. Although the British bombardment had silenced most of the German artillery, the deep dugouts were intact and Fricourt was defended almost entirely by machine gun and rifle fire. The Middlesex attack lost its momentum and small groups of men tried their best to get forward, the dead and wounded, totalling nearly 500, lying in No Man's Land. Some 40 men of the Middx. were to reach the Sunken Road.

This large shell failed to do its deadly work and lies by the side of the Ferme du Bois.

Behind the Middlesex were the 10/Yorks. & Lancs whose orders were originally to advance just behind the creeping barrage and pass through the leading battalion towards Bottom Wood and Quadrangle Trench, their ultimate objective. Reports of heavy losses by the Middlesex and the S.L.I. brought about a change of orders and the 10/Yorks & Lancs were ordered forward at 8.40am to consolidate the first gains. This was quickly achieved and they continued as far as the Sunken Road. Any further advance was, at the moment, impossible against the machine gun fire from Fricourt village and wood.

The 8/S.L.I. on the immediate left of the Middlesex, sustained heavy losses on leaving their trench but reached the first enemy line. From here, bombers cleared the way along the communication trenches and the Somersets arrived at the support trench and continued towards the Sunken Road. The 8/Lincoln moving up in support was held up for a time by German bombers but joined the leading battalion and together they occupied Lozenge Alley on the west of the junction with the main road. The alley then run east to Fricourt Farm and a party tried to work its way towards the farm but was repulsed. Another party of the 8/Lincoln successfully advanced north and entered Crucifix Trench near the Crucifix from which the trench takes its name.

The Germans were now counter attacking to gain the lost ground. They obviously wanted to retake possession of the Sunken Road and bombers approached up Lonely Trench to find that parties of the Yorks & Lancs had completely blocked the trench with sandbags. The Royal Engineers of 98th Field Coy. were sent to help consolidation and in fact were in action with the other battalions against the German counter attacks.

The 10/W. Yorks of the 50th Brigade were to advance westwards on a front of 550 meters to provide flank cover for a later attack on Fricourt village by the 7/Green Howards of the same Brigade. The two leading companies made excellent progress at first, crossing the first German trench with little difficulty before the Germans had time to get organised. The Yorkshiremen then hastened towards Red Cottage, situated at the northern extremity of Fricourt. The rear companies, on starting their advance, met stiff opposition from the now organised defences and intense fire from Fricourt and the German Tambour, just south of the triple Tambour mine, caused devastating losses. The men lay dead in attack formation and just a few of the lucky survivors managed to reach the German front line where they remained until nightfall. Meanwhile, the two leading companies were at Red Cottage. With no support they were isolated and were eventually repulsed by German counter attacks later in the morning, a few groups escaping to join the 10/Yorks & Lancs, the right hand battalion of the 63rd Brigade. No Man's Land was

The last remnants of the German concrete protection of the well at Fricourt Farm. It can be imagined how useful it was to have drinking water to hand, for during the long British bombardment prior to the attack it was impossible to bring supplies food and water up to the German trenches

constantly swept by six machine guns and it was found impossible to support the rear companies of the mutilated West Yorks.

Due to the huge losses of the 7/West Yorks, the 7/Green Howards could not advance as planned and the 7/East Yorks took over the West Yorkshire positions and their fire assisted in keeping the enemy down. The 7/Green Howards had only three companies, the fourth had attacked erroneously at 7.45am and was virtually annihilated within a few minutes by a single machine gun.

Preceded by a short artillery bombardment, the three companies of the 7/Green Howards began their attack at 2.30pm, not without a certain degree of anxiety, now having no flank in the north to protect them against the very strongest of the Fricourt defences between Wing Corner and the German Tambour. The artillery action had been ineffective, there being many dud shells with the result that there were only four small gaps in the wire, all well covered by enemy fire. Covered by Lewis gun fire the three companies went over the top to be met by devastating machine gun and rifle fire, many Germans standing on the parapet. Half of the men were down before covering fifty yards. A few small groups reached the village where they were quickly killed or taken prisoner. It appears a few men managed to shelter in a cellar but most lay in No Man's Land waiting for dark in order to return to safety.

At 8.30am the 7/East Yorks which had taken over the frontage of the Middlesex, commenced their attack. The inevitable result ensued. The two leading companies had 150 casualties in the first few yards of their advance. It was impossible to cross No Man's Land. By 3.00pm the 6/Dorset and the rear companies of the 7/East Yorks had been brought up and were ordered to attack but this order was cancelled in order to allow the depleted 50th Brigade to be replaced by the 51st.

It will be seen in the next section that the 22nd Brigade of the 7th Division successfully performed its flank attack on the east side of Fricourt. This, along with the success of the 64th Brigade had gone exactly according to plan, but the attack in the centre had failed and in the evening, the Germans were still in Fricourt. Events were to prove that the pincer movement had rendered the village untenable and the Germans evacuated the village during the night of 1st/2nd July, leaving a small rear guard to cover their retreat to their next line of defence. The Official History records casualties of 4,256 in the 21st Division and 1,155 in the 50th Brigade. The 10/West Yorks casualties were 710 officers and men, the highest loss in any single battalion on the 1st July. The West Yorkshiremen who had shed their blood so freely would never know their sacrifice had not been in vain.

Objective 12
Mametz, Pommiers Redoubt

Battalions Engaged

Corps	Div.	Brig.	Bn.No.	Battalion
XV	7	20	8	Devons
XV	7	20	9	Devons
XV	7	20	2	Border
XV	7	20	2	Gordon Highlanders
XV	7	22	2	Royal Warwicks
XV	7	22	20	Manchesters - 5th Manchester Pals
XV	7	22	1	Royal Welsh Fusiliers
XV	7	22	2	Royal Irish
XV	7	91	2	Queen's
XV	7	91	1	South Staffs
XV	7	91	21	Manchesters - 6th Manchester Pals
XV	7	91	22	Manchesters - 7th Manchester Pals
XV	7	0	24	Manchesters - Oldham Pals (pioneers)

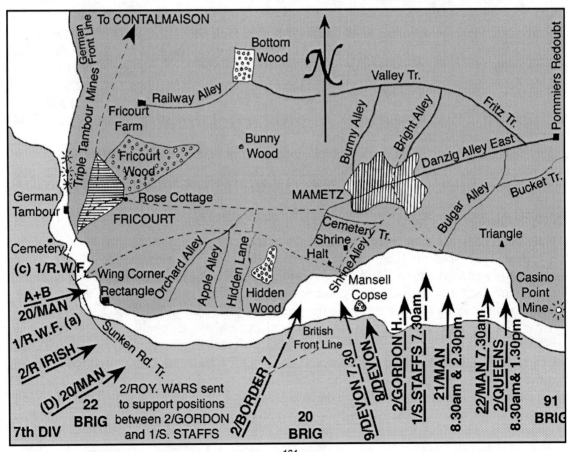

Mametz, one of the many small villages which became a household name and part of history during the battle of the Somme, is on the D64 between Fricourt and Montauban. The village was well fortified and completely surrounded by a system of trenches. A little to the east was Pommiers Redoubt while towards Fricourt were the defences described in the previous section. The 7th Division, with its 20th and 91st Brigades was to attack Mametz while the 22nd Brigade's objective was the attack on the eastern flank of Fricourt to complete the pincer movement with the 21st Division on its left.

Four Russian saps had been excavated to the German front line and in order to avoid casualties, the assault battalions of the 20th and 91st Brigades were assembled in the support trenches.

Prior to zero hour, the leading battalions of the 91st Brigade, the 22/Manchester with the 1/South Staffs on its left moved forward through the Russian saps, opened up at the last moment and almost immediately had seized and passed over the German front trench. From here, the ground rose and both battalions lost heavily through fire from Mametz and Danzig Alley. The advance continued and within fifteen minutes the Staffordshiremen were in Cemetery Trench just south of the village, having covered a distance of 650 meters. At 8.00am the Manchesters entered Bucket Trench to the east of Mametz and close to Danzig Alley East. By now the Staffords had entered the southern end of the ruined village and German resistance was weakening. A good number of prisoners were escorted to the rear. However, German units in strongpoints in the west and north fought tenaciously and the brilliant advance of the Staffords came to a halt. A few dug in and remained in the village but most had to retire to Cemetery Trench. An hour or so later three companies of the 21/Manchester went forward to support the Staffords but the combined battalions could not get forward towards the village. At the same time two companies of the 2/Queens reinforced the 22/Manchester in Bucket Trench and Bulgar Alley but fire from Danzig Alley East prevented further advance at the moment. When news came that Pommiers Redoubt had fallen in the 18th Division's

Lonely Copse, just north of Fricourt and west of Fricourt Wood was an obstacle on the left of the 10/West Yorks and 1/E. Yorks 50th brigade on their advance to Red Cottage. Fricourt Church is on the right.

sector to the right, a thirty minute bombardment was made west from Pommiers Redoubt to crush the remaining obstacles in Mametz and break the German communications from Danzig Alley towards Montauban. The last two companies of the Queens went forward and at 1.00pm, had entered Danzig Alley East pushing the defenders to the north of the village or towards Fritz Trench and Bright Alley. The latter was entered by bombing parties. The advance had now picked up its former élan and the Queens entered Fritz Trench. Following the bombardment the South Staffs and the 21/Manchester were able to advance from Cemetery Trench and again entered the southern end of the village from where they cleared pockets of enemy resistance at the western extremity of the village. Apart from some opposition in the north, Mametz was in the hands of the 91st Brigade.

The 20th Brigade's advance was in the shape of a "V". The right to attack on the western outskirts of Mametz, the centre in a north easterly direction right of Hidden Wood towards Willow Avenue and the left towards Hidden Wood and beyond. Four small mines had been fired in the cratered area between the 20th and 22nd Brigade's frontage in an attempt to destroy known German positions. The Gordon Highlanders were then to join the 9/Devon and advance on Bunny Alley and Orchard Alley. Apple Alley, which runs south off Orchard alley was the initial objective of the 2/Border. The right companies of the Gordon Highlanders adjacent to the 1/South Stafford of the 91st Brigade leaped into the German front line trench as the enemy was mounting its defences and was quickly overrun. The left company was held up by concealed wire suffering heavy casualties before reaching the front line. During the long British bombardment many shells had failed to explode due to faulty fuses and dud shells were scattered over a wide area. At zero hour the 9/Devon moved forward and was caught by devastating machine gun fire from the Shrine in Mametz civil cemetery, from Mametz village and from Fricourt Wood. Captain D.L. Martin one of the company commanders of the 9/Devon had predicted such an event. While on leave in England, he had constructed a plasticine model of his attack area and forecast his men would be prone to severe enemy

The view from a German machine gun post near the Shrine in Mametz civil cemetery. The 8 and 9/Devons (20th Brigade) were particularly hard hit as they left the shelter of Mansell Copse in the centre of the picture. Captain Martin had predicted such a result and fell with many of his men.

The uphill line of attack of the 18th Division towards the Pommiers Redoubt on the horizon. The photograph was taken from the site of the Casino Point Mine.

fire from the Shrine. His fears were well founded and he fell with many of his men on the exposed slope after Mansell Copse. The Devons did not falter and after entering the German front line, they went forward a further 250 meters to the support trench. Not being able to advance further, they set about clearing the support and communication trenches and some prisoners were escorted to the rear. This done, they offered fire support to the flank battalions who had managed to get ahead. Two companies of the 8/Devon were sent forward to assist but sustained heavy losses in No Man's Land. The remainder joined the 9/Devon and the Highlanders in the support trench. Within thirty minutes the leading companies were passing the Halt and into Shrine Alley. Enemy resistance stiffened and another machine gun to the south east of Mametz on the Maricourt road caused heavy casualties. Some of the Gordons and 9/Devon spent most of the morning clearing up the troublesome German defences. The remainder of the Gordons were unable to continue past Shrine Alley but were in contact with the 1/South Staffs (91st Brigade) in Cemetery Trench. The 2/Border on the left was able to get forward with less difficulty having some protection from the physical features of the ground and within a short time had crossed the front line and was advancing on Hidden Lane to the west of Hidden Wood, only 140 meters from its final objective, Apple Alley. Bombing and bayonetting their way forward, clearing up pockets of resistance, they cleared Hidden Wood and reached Apple Alley. They had quickly reached their objective and found themselves too far ahead with no flank support - both the Devons and Gordon Highlanders having been held up. About 1.00pm the remaining company of the 8th Devons was sent up to take position between its sister battalion and the Highlanders.

Two companies of the 2/Royal Warwick in reserve were sent to fill the gap between the Highlanders and the 1/South Stafford. At 3.30pm. with the remainder of the 8/Devon, the battalions moved forward and the last of the German resistance crumbled in Mametz and the Shrine. Some two hundred prisoners were taken. Half an hour later all resistance in the northern part of the village was subdued and the whole of Mametz was now under the control of the 7th Division. By the early evening the 2/Queens had cleared Fritz Trench. The centre and right had been a complete success and the new gains were consolidated. The defences in Mametz were repaired and consolidated in order to deal with any counter attack.

The 22nd Brigade's flanking attack on Fricourt was undertaken by the 20/Manchester with two companies of the 1/Royal Welsh Fusiliers. They were quickly over the German front line but afterwards fire from a distant machine gun caused many casualties. The same gun virtually destroyed the bombing parties. The Rectangle was entered by a few of the Manchesters but they could not hold and retired to the support line. The Welsh Fusiliers enjoyed better success, bombing their way both sides of the Rectangle and up the Sunken Road Trench to the outskirts of Fricourt, thus allowing the Manchesters to get forward. Meanwhile, A Company of the Welsh Fusiliers had advanced to the strongpoint Wing Corner while C Company was to the south of Fricourt cemetery. The 2/Royal Irish were in divisional reserve.

The 22nd Brigade had achieved all its objectives and the flanking manoeuvre on the east of Fricourt was completed.

The attack by the 7th Division was an outstanding success, all objectives having been taken. Casualties amounted to 3,480 officers and men, the third lowest of all the attack Divisions.

Objective 13
The Attack East of Mametz
& West of Montauban

Battalions Engaged

Corps	Div.	Brig.	Bn.No.	Battalion
XIII	18	53	8	Norfolks
XIII	18	53	6	Royal Berks
XIII	18	53	10	Essex
XIII	18	53	8	Suffolks
XIII	18	54	11	Royal Fusiliers
XIII	18	54	7	Bedfords
XIII	18	54	6	Northamptons
XIII	18	54	12	Middlesex
XIII	18	55	7	Queen's
XIII	18	55	7	Buffs
XIII	18	55	8	East Surreys
XIII	18	55	7	Royal West Kents
XIII	18	0	8	Royal Sussex (pioneers)

Objective 14
The Attack on Montauban Village

Battalions Engaged

Corps	Div.	Brig.	Bn.No.	Battalion
XIII	30	21	18	King's - 2nd Liverpool Pals
XIII	30	21	19	Manchesters - 4th Manchester Pals
XIII	30	21	2	Wilts
XIII	30	21	2	Green Howards
XIII	30	89	17	King's - 1st Liverpool Pals
XIII	30	89	19	King's - 3rd Liverpool Pals
XIII	30	89	20	King's - 4th Liverpool Pals
XIII	30	89	2	Bedfords
XIII	30	90	2	Royal Scots Fusiliers
XIII	30	90	16	Manchesters - 1st Manchester Pals
XIII	30	90	17	Manchesters - 2nd Manchester Pals
XIII	30	90	18	Manchesters - 3rd Manchester Pals
XIII	30	0	11	South Lancs (pioneers)

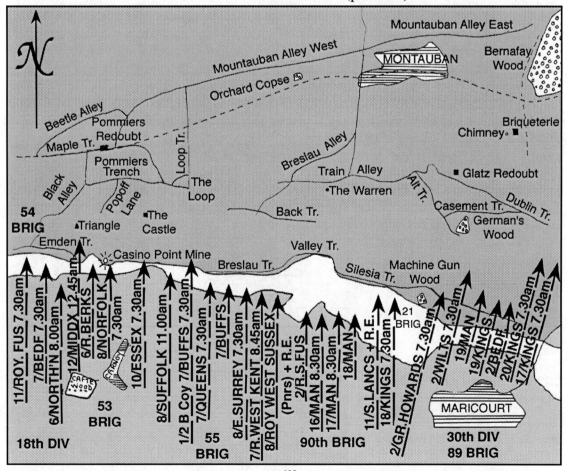

The 18th (Eastern) and 30th Divisions of the XIII Corps with the 9th (Scottish) Division in reserve were facing the area between Mametz and Montauban. The 18th Division was to attack the area between the two villages while the 30th Division was assigned the assault on Montauban itself. The right hand battalion of the 30th Division was adjacent to units of the French XX Corps, carrying the sobriquet "Iron Corps" from its exploits at Verdun, which had taken over the sector further to the south and east.

Observers on Maricourt ridge enjoyed a good view of the German positions and were able to direct the artillery, deployed in relative safety on the reverse slope of the same ridge. The Germans had prepared several lines of front and support trenches behind which the newly constructed Pommiers Trench, Train Alley and Dublin Trench protected the approach to the Montauban road. Amongst the forward defences Glatz Redoubt and The Castle were strategically placed. Montauban itself was well fortified on the east, west and southern perimeters while to the north the long Montauban Alley ran along the reverse slopes of Caterpillar Valley from Montauban to Pommiers Redoubt, a strongpoint some 1300 meters east of Mametz. This was the German 1st Position. From Maurepas, travelling north west through Guillemont and Longueval and extending west towards the two Bazentins (Petit and Grand), the Germans had prepared a very strong 2nd Position from where reinforcements could be sent to the south if necessary.

The British artillery with the French guns on the right had performed to a high degree of accuracy, putting out of action almost all the German artillery emplacements. The German wire was glistening in the morning sun and could be seen for the most part, to be very well cut. These signs augured well for the waiting infantry.

The 89th and 21st Brigades of the 30th Division had taken up their positions during the evening of 30th June and at 7.28am the following morning, a hurricane bombardment by Stokes mortars was directed against the forward German positions. At 7.30am the leading battalions of the 89th Brigade, the 17/King's on the right and its sister battalion, the 20th on the left advanced quickly over the 450 meters of No Man's Land with little opposition. The 17/King's had passed over Favière Trench, then to the right of German's Wood and had entered Casement Trench by 8.00am. The 20/King's, keeping pace, were in Alt Trench. There was a

The headstone of Capt. W.P. Nevill of the 8/East Surrys who was killed leading his men kicking footballs across No Mans Land to the East of Casino Point Mine. He is buried in Carnoy Military Cemetery.

delightful illustration of allied co-operation when the Commanding Officer of the 17/King's advanced with the second wave arm-in-arm with his counterpart from the 3rd Battalion of the 153rd French Regiment.

Both the King's had now caught up with the creeping barrage and rested a few minutes after their energetic advance. The 2/Bedford and some of the 19/King's were in close support and captured 300 prisoners and 4 machine guns. As the prisoners were being escorted to the rear they collected a further group of Germans who had surrendered to the leading battalions at German's Wood. The prisoners looked physically strained and tired, possibly through the strain of the bombardment, lack of food supplies and they offered little resistance. The King's set off again and, at 8.30am, had entered Dublin Trench, their first objective. The artillery barrage had so damaged the trench that it was unusable and it was not surprising the King's found it unoccupied. The support battalions brought up equipment and a new trench was dug parallel to Dublin Trench but a little further to the north. The 20/King's were now close to Glatz Redoubt.

The 19/Manchester and 18/King's led the 21st Brigade's attack north towards Glatz Redoubt. Like the 89th Brigade, they advanced rapidly and crossed Silesia Trench, the Manchesters losses being light but the King's on the left were caught by fire from a hidden machine gun. They arrived at Alt Trench ahead of the barrage and waited until it had passed. At 7.45am both battalions occupied the trench. Fire from Train Alley and The Warren prevented any further movement and caused many casualties in the leading battalions. The 2/Green Howards lost 200 men while crossing No Man's Land to support the weakened King's. On arrival at Alt Trench, the support battalion was sent with bombs to counter the Germans who, recovering a little from the initial shock, were now out of the dug-outs and were sending bombers to the east. There ensued a bitter bombing contest between the antagonists, the Green Howards emerging as victors, scattering or killing the enemy bombers. This enabled the 18/King's to rush Train Alley and silence the machine gun which had caused so much damage. However, fire from The Warren, untaken by the 18th Division on the left, still accomplished its deadly work and the 2/Wiltshire, engaged mainly in carrying up supplies, lost almost a hundred men. The 19/Manchester and 18/King's were now able to link up with the leading battalions of the 89th Brigade and entered Glatz Redoubt which was found to be in ruins, apparently having been hit by a large shell.

The way was now open for the 90th Brigade to pass through the gains of the 21st and 89th Brigades and make their attack on Montauban. At 8.30am the leading battalions, the 16th and 17th Manchesters advanced in comparative safety up Railway Valley to the east of Talus Boisé, aided also by a smoke screen laid by the other two brigades. Leaving this cover, they came under fire from Breslau Alley but pushed forward and reached Train Alley. Like their comrades in the other brigades they caught up with the British barrage and were obliged to halt. The forward companies sheltered in Train Alley while the rear, along with the 2/Royal Scots Fusiliers in close support, took what cover they could in the open cratered ground. The British barrage caused many casualties during the enforced halt and the wait must have seemed interminable. However, at this time, the German machine gun in Breslau Alley was spotted and eventually put out of action by a Lewis gun of the 16/Manchester.

The 55th Brigade of the 18th Division could not reach their objective which left the left flank of the 90th Brigade badly exposed to enfilade fire. Under cover of a very dense smoke screen laid from Glatz Redoubt, the Manchesters and Royal Scots Fusiliers moved forward towards the village. Apart from fire from a single machine gun from the ruins at the start, there was no further opposition and at 10.05am they found the village deserted. With emotions high, they moved to the north of the village, the Fusiliers passing up Valley Trench with the 17/Manchesters on their right and the 16th on the left, doing their best to keep abreast, and the victorious battalions entered the eastern end of Montauban Alley, their final objective. The German occupants surrendered without opposition and hundreds more were seen retreating north along the road to Bazentin le Grand to their 2nd Position. The British artillery was turned on the retreating Germans. The 16/Manchester rushed the last remnants of the German field artillery and returned triumphantly with three of the guns.

It was essential to prepare strongpoints in the village in preparation for any counter attack and three sections of the 201st Field Coy. R.E., the 11/South Lancs (Pioneers) and the Royal Scots Fusiliers set about this task. Supplies of necessary material as well as hot food were brought up by the 18/Manchester. It was quiet for some while allowing consolidation to continue unimpaired. Another section of Royal Engineers was sent up to help in the urgent work. In the early afternoon the German artillery further to the north laid an accurate and continuous barrage on the village which caused considerable casualties. The barrage ended between 4.00 and 5.00pm.

There still remained the taking of La Briqueterie with its tall chimney serving as a very useful observation post and the fall of Montauban offered the opportunity to attack this stronghold. The heavy artillery commenced an hour long bombardment after which the 4th Company of the 20/King's delivered its attack, while a bombing party approached from Dublin Alley to cut off any retreat from the stronghold. The barrage was entirely

The German Front Line on 1st July was situated almost entirely on high ground and the view here on the left is the uphill line of attack of the 53 and 55 Brigades of the 18th Division towards the Mametz-Montauban road. The 30th Division was in a position to the right of the Carnoy-Montauban road ready for their successful attack on Montauban.

successful, destroying most of the outbuildings and the King's rushed forward to find many German dead and they took control of La Briqueterie. The only resistance was a last ditch stand from a hurriedly mounted machine gun which caused some casualties but this too, was stormed and the defenders were overwhelmed. The 30th Division, flushed with success wished to continue towards Bernafay and Trones Wood towards Guillemont but the Commanding Officer, Major-General J.S.M. Shea was not allowed to engage his men. However, patrols were sent out later to Bernafay Wood which was found to be empty apart from a few Germans who were taken prisoner. Not being included in the plan for the day, no attempt was made to consolidate it.

Turning our attention to the left wing of XIII Corps, the 18th Division had three brigades in line; from left to right, the 54th, 53rd and 55th, the latter being adjacent to the 21st Brigade of the 30th Division. Arriving in March, they had been involved in mining activities in No Man's Land which had, as a result, become quite cratered covering a width of about 140 meters. The Germans who had occupied the craters retired to the support line after laying wire and spiked stakes in the front line. However, some Germans remained and set up machine guns and sniper positions amongst the craters which were to prove serious obstacles to the 18th Division.

The 53rd Brigade was to clear the cratered area with the help of a flame-thrower, the other two brigades were to pass either side of the craters. The 183rd Tunnelling Company had prepared two mines (5,000 and 300 lbs.) under the German parapet at Casino Point, just to the south of Mine Trench. These were fired at 7.27am with the aim of destroying the dug-outs and machine gun posts.

The 6/Royal Berks and the 8/Norfolk formed the vanguard of the 53rd Brigade and the leading companies advanced with few difficulties at the start, helped by the firing of the two mines and the flame-thrower on their right. The wire being well cut, the men were quickly across the front and support lines before coming under fire from The Castle, directly in front of them and from Back Trench slightly to their right. The Castle was quickly overrun but the defences in Back Trench were a more serious obstacle, the right of the Norfolks coming under continuous fire. The left of the Norfolks along with the Berkshires were less affected and they continued towards Pommiers Trench where they were met by fire from three machine guns. Approaching up Popoff Lane, a bombing party seized one of the guns. The other two, surprised by the attack from the flank, retired with their guns in the direction of Pommiers Redoubt. This permitted entry into Pommiers Trench which was occupied at 7.50am. Fire from The Loop at the eastern end of Pommiers Trench prevented further movement towards their next objective, Pommiers Redoubt, the Royal Berkshires suffering heavy casualties. A company of the 10/Essex was sent forward in support. The Loop held out against bombers and Lewis guns, the Germans having blocked the end of Pommiers Trench with wire. The same obstacle faced bombing parties trying to approach Pommiers Redoubt.

The 11/Royal Fusiliers and 7/Bedford led the attack of the 54th Brigade on the left. Like the 53rd Brigade, they crossed the front and support lines without difficulty but on leaving Emden Trench towards the German third line, fire from The Triangle caused heavy losses to the leading companies of the Bedfords. The strongpoint was rushed and silenced; the men continuing to within a short distance of Pommiers Trench. Here, they had to halt having caught up with the British creeping barrage. At 7.50, when the barrage had lifted, aided by two of their own machine guns, they entered Pommiers Trench with the 53rd Brigade on their right. Meanwhile, the Fusiliers on the left cleared the craters and communication trenches needed to get supplies through.

The 54th and 53rd Brigades were now linked and their next objectives were Maple Trench, the route to Pommiers Redoubt and Beetle Alley beyond. The Queen's on the right and part of the Norfolks were still delayed by fire from Breslau Support Trench. The Loop, still untaken, prevented any assistance from the other battalions.

At 8.30am a frontal attack was made on the redoubt but was met by heavy fire and it was quickly realised it could not be taken frontally. The Royal Fusiliers equipped with Lewis guns succeeded in forcing an entry into Maple Trench from where they opened fire on Pommiers Redoubt killing many of the defenders on the parapet. The Fusiliers immediately rushed through the gaps in the wire, took complete control of Maple Trench and with the men facing the redoubt, charged forward and after a bitter hand to hand struggle with no quarter being given or taken, the Germans were killed or taken prisoner.

At 9.00am, A Company of the 6/Northants. moved forward in support and the mixed battalions continued their advance north and bombed their way into Beetle Alley. From here, an attempt was made to advance east along Montauban Alley but the alley was well blocked and the bombers were held up.

The leading battalions of the 55th Brigade, the 7/Queen's and the 8/East Surrey crossed into No Man's Land, some 200 meters wide at this point and although the flame thrower to the west had subdued resistance to its front, fire from the eastern side of No Man's Land caused heavy casualties in the Queen's battalion. Captain W.P. Nevill of the 8/East Surrey led his four platoons over the top, each platoon kicking a football towards the front line for the honour of scoring the first "Goal". Nevill was killed but his platoons continued the advance. Two of the footballs were retrieved; one is in the National Army Museum and the other in the Queen's Regimental Museum at Howe Barracks, Canterbury in Kent.

A company of the 7/Buffs was sent forward but was unable to penetrate the area and the advance was held up. At 8.45am the 7/Royal West Kent moved forward in support following the path of the Queens, but they too, suffered heavy casualties from the same source. The 8/East Surrey was delayed in No Man's Land between the front and support line by fire from The Warren, just south of Train Alley. This stronghold was not taken until the 30th Division was able to concentrate fire on it from Glatz Redoubt and Train Alley. The 7/East Surrey, supported by two companies of the 7/Buffs could now get forward towards their first objective, Train Alley. The remaining companies of the West Kents moved forward to support the Surreys and Buffs and by noon had arrived at the Montauban road.

With the 30th Division in Montauban and parts of Montauban Alley East, the 18th Division in the Pommiers Redoubt and Montauban Alley West, the German strongpoints Breslau Support Trench and The Loop were almost isolated with no means of retreat. The Queen's secured the former with hand grenades while the Norfolks took The Loop bringing in some sixty prisoners with them. There was still resistance from Back Trench which the Germans refused to concede. It was attacked by bombers from three sides but the courageous enemy held out until 2.00pm when, at last, the garrison surrendered.

Meanwhile the remainder of Montauban Alley had been secured, from the east by the 30th Division and from the west by the 18th. Patrols sent north of Montauban Alley towards Caterpillar Wood saw the Germans retreating north.

After 5.00pm the whole area was quiet with little fire on either side enabling the wounded to be brought in and fresh supplies brought up. Roads and railtrack were repaired and field batteries brought forward. The patrols north of Montauban could see in front of them Caterpillar Wood, part of Mametz Wood, Bernafay and Trones Wood and, on the horizon the village of Longueval and the dark menacing shapes of Delville Wood and High Wood. They would not know the names of these places, destined like the village they had just taken, to be engraved forever in our history.

The casualties of the 30th and 18th Divisions were 3,011 and 3,115 respectively. Taking into consideration that most of the German artillery had been put out of action by the British bombardment and the rapidity of the advance of the infantry, the number of casualties appears to be heavy. This underlines what damage a few well-placed machine guns can do to infantry advancing over open ground. Even so, the XIII corps suffered the least casualties of the day with all objectives taken. This was indeed welcome news not only for General Rawlinson at the head of the Fourth Army, but for General Haig in supreme command, for the British Government and the British people at home.

THE CASUALTIES

The term "casualties" means those who were killed in action or died of wounds, wounded, missing or taken prisoner.

This sunny first day of July which had promised so much for the participants turned out, as has been recorded in this guide, to be a day of tragic circumstances. Casualties are determined by the absence of soldiers at the roll call. The initial figures were almost 62,000 due to the uncertainty of the fate of the large number of dead and wounded, or simply missing in No Man's Land. Bringing in the wounded was a dangerous operation for the stretcher bearers. The Germans were not disposed, except in very few cases, to allow the collection of the wounded and many had to wait until nightfall to try to return. During this time many died from their wounds. Subsequently, the casualty figures were corrected as the fate of the men became known.

The following two tables show the original casualty estimates and the later amended figures:-

	ORIGINAL ESTIMATES	FINAL FIGURES
Killed or died of wounds	8,170	19,240
Wounded	35,888	35,493
Missing	17,758	2,152
Prisoners of War	—	585
Total	61,816	57,470

The figures show that 11,000 of the missing in the original estimates were either killed on the day of battle or subsequently died of their wounds. Figures in the southern sector where the objectives were taken were easier to ascertain. However, in the north, particularly at Serre which remained in German hands throughout the campaign, corpses

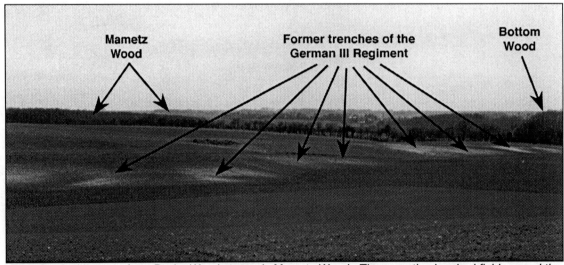

The view looking east from Peake Woods towards Mametz Wood. The recently ploughed fields reveal the excavations of the German III Regiment

were rotting on the wire throughout the summer. A large number of infantry were literally blown to pieces by the German artillery in No Man's Land. The divisional losses listed north to south and taken from the Official History are recorded below:-

DIVISION	CASUALTIES	OBJECTIVE
46th (North Midland)	2,455	Gommecourt
56th (London)	4,314	Gommecourt
31st	3,600	Serre
48th (South Midland) 2 bns.	1,060	Serre
4th	4,692	Redan Ridge
29th	5,240	Beaumont Hamel
36th (Ulster)	5,104	Schwaben Redoubt
49th (West Riding) 5 bns.	590	Thiepval
32nd	3,949	Thiepval
8th	5,121	Ovillers
34th	6,380	La Boisselle
21st	4,256	SW of Contalmaison
17th (Northern)		
3 bns. of 50th Brig.	1,115	Fricourt
7th	3,410	Mametz
18th (Eastern)	3,115	E of Mametz
30th	3,011	Montauban

A look at the divisional figures shows that even where success was complete - the attack on Montauban for example - casualties were in excess of 3,000. The highest recorded casualties are those incurred by the 34th Division. All twelve battalions of the 101st, 102nd and 103rd Brigades and the pioneers were engaged against a strong German defence near the main road to Bapaume. All divisions north of the main road suffered heavy losses - the 36th (Ulster), 29th and 8th Divisions all had losses in excess of 5,000, three divisions had over 4,000 and five divisions sustained casualties of over 3,000.

With the advantage of today's technology, it is perhaps somewhat difficult to imagine the fighting on this first day of the battle. This was no push-button nuclear war aided by the latest advances in technology, transport and communication, but a personal war where the infantryman, if he managed to survive the horrendous fire from German machine guns and artillery, survived or died through the use of his rifle, his bayonet or simply with his bare hands. He saw his friends and the Germans fall and die on the field of battle. Dismembered bodies lay everywhere. The horror he witnessed marked him for the remainder of his life. Some never recovered.

This then was the result of the Big Push. Many of the survivors felt almost a sense of guilt at being alive after seeing their friends cut down in their hundreds. The cream of British youth had died and whole communities were in deep mourning. This was just the first day of a four and half month struggle on the Somme. There was no option but to continue the battle. The commanders reconsidered strategy and tactics, the losses replaced, the survivors prepared themselves to continue the struggle and the killing fields of the Somme were to claim over half a million British and Empire casualties before the campaign ended in a sea of mud in November.

CONCLUSION

Much has been written about the failure, partial and complete success of the actions on the 1st July and a thorough review of these theories is outside the scope of this guide due to limitations of space. However, it is felt some comment on the day's events is necessary and the following represents but a brief summary.

In spite of the meticulous preparations and the week-long bombardment, most divisions were in difficulty as soon as they left the trenches, particularly from Gommecourt to Ovillers. The artillery barrage failed to cut the German wire in many places and did little damage to the deep German fortifications. The fault cannot be placed entirely on the artillery - they had the correct range but there were many dud shells. Later a modified wire cutting shell was used more successfully. The chalky terrain in the Thiepval area absorbed to a great extent the repercussion of the initial explosion and the deep German dug-outs remained mostly intact. The sheer noise of the barrage comforted the waiting British infantry and no doubt, put terror in the hearts of the Germans. At 7.30am precisely the barrage was lifted and the artillery began its preparations to lengthen its range in accordance with Rawlinson's plan. Although silence reigned, the mens' ears were still ringing as they left the trenches. The Germans, also numbed and dazed from the long barrage, left their dug-outs and angrily mounted their machine guns. They could not believe the sight before them, wave after wave of heavily laden infantry advancing as though on parade to the wire where they desperately tried to cut a way through. They were a perfect target for the German gunners and this tragic story was repeated a long way down the line.

Various ways were conceived of ensuring the communication system would allow accurate progress reports of the attacking infantry. These ranged from reports from the air, by telephone, reflective patches attached to the backs of soldiers, the use of pigeons and, in the last resort, by runner. As the British artillery lengthened its range, the German artillery laid a barrage on No Man's Land from which the smoke and bursting shells impaired visibility. Communication cables were destroyed, repaired and destroyed again. The forward observation officers were unable to see exactly what was happening. A typical example was at Serre where men were seen to be entering the village. The village was reported to be in British hands when in fact, the few soldiers who had penetrated the outskirts of the village were not seen again. Due to poor communications, several days passed before Rawlinson was aware of even an estimate of the casualties. There is no place for pessimism in an army commander and his A.D.C.'s tended rather to keep him informed of the success from Fricourt to Montauban rather than pay much attention to the stories of thousands of wounded men who somehow had managed to crawl back to the British front line and using words like *"murder, horror, never again"* The early morning mist on the first of July was quickly cleared by the rising run and the temperature soared to 72 degrees F. For many of the 35,500 wounded, it was a terrible day. Lying there with no shelter from the sun and quickly out of drinking water, many died from their wounds or loss of blood. The wounded tried to crawl to the comparative safety of a shell hole. The less seriously wounded moved inch by inch towards the British line, ever fearful of German snipers who were still in a state of killing ecstasy. Those who made it back to the front line needed care and many were in urgent need of transport, usually by rail, to distant hospitals. The arrangements for such evacuation were woefully inadequate. The long obituary lists gradually began to appear in the newspapers and those northern towns who formed their own Pals and other battalions were particularly hard hit - hardly a household was spared from news of a death, wounded or missing soldier. The heavy losses were replaced by good men but the very nature and camaraderie of the Pals battalions, composed of men who had worked together in peace time and fought together on the Somme, were never to be the same again.

The very scale of the British attack inevitably meant that some gains would be made and some would say it was a victory but as many would say it was a pyrrhic victory. Haig and Rawlinson differed on many issues and Rawlinson usually had his way. Both men held the same rank of General but it was Haig who was the Commander in Chief and the latter has been the subject of some criticism for ceding to his subordinate's wishes. Rawlinson's plan of attack was too rigid and left no room for any individual initiative of officers, N.C.O.'s or men and this, in itself, was partly responsible for the horrendous casualties. Haig would have preferred a quick dash across No-Man's-Land to gain some element of surprise by the attacking infantry. In Haig's view, it was absolutely essential for the troops to be in the enemy front line trench before the Germans could mount their guns. But Rawlinson, ever optimistic in the efficacy of the British bombardment, instructed an orderly, almost parade-like advance towards the German front line. There were also differences between the British and the French, the former wishing to attack at dawn while the French insisted the attack should start at 7.30am. Haig, always sensitive to the wishes of the French, gave way.

The German view of the events on the 1st July was that the British soldier did not lack courage, but lacked training, experience and showed little initiative. There is some truth in this statement, Rawlinson's rigid plan allowing no room for personal initiative. The German soldiers were, for the most part, much better trained and many were hardened fighting men. The attack by the British in thick formation stood no chance against the undestroyed German defences.

The French divisions had achieved 80% success on the right wing and had taken far more prisoners than their British counterparts and there was some French criticism of the British performance. Some divisional commanders were either dismissed or transferred out of the sector.

Mametz and Montauban were quickly taken by the 7th, 18th and 30th Divisions but no order was received to improve this situation. Permission was sought to enter Mametz Wood, but this was refused. It was to prove a costly error of judgement, the 38th Division suffered heavy casualties before finally being in control of the wood a few days later. Bernafay Wood and almost all of Trones Wood were unoccupied and could have been entered and consolodated, but no order was received. Trones Wood in particular was to be the scene of bitter wood fighting between the 8th and 14th July by the 30th, 9th and 18th Divisions. These costly attacks on well defended woods were amongst the very worst conditions in which soldiers are asked to fight.

With the benefit of hindsight we can sit back and reflect on the results of the first day of the battle but Haig and Rawlinson had no such advantage and in the evening they were not too disappointed with the results of the day's work. Haig had predicted heavy casualties. Both have been heavily censured by public opinion for the manner in which the battle was conducted. A year later, Arthur Conan Doyle in his summary of the 1st

July attack wrote, "These young lives were gladly laid down as a price for final victory - and history may show that it was really on those Picardy slopes that final victory was in truth ensured" [The British Campaign in France and Flanders, 1916, Arthur Conan Doyle, page 101, Hodder & Stoughton, 1918]. Penned in 1917 with victory not yet in sight, the words ring with patriotism and optimism.

The necessary optimism of the senior commanders was not always shared by the infantry, particularly the wounded and survivors who had witnessed the most unimaginable horrors. No-one can know the thoughts of the nineteen thousand dead prior to being cut down in the prime of youth.

It was Haig and Rawlinson's lot to continue the struggle and in fairness to Rawlinson, who had been the butt of so much criticism, it must be said that this was redeemed to some extent by his planning and success of the attack on the 14th July. What then had been achieved? Britain had responded to France's call for help and no further German reinforcements were sent to the Meuse front and thus, Verdun was saved. The mass of regulars, volunteers and territorials had been put to the test and many lessons had been learned. Some gains had been made and the Germans had been mauled but not broken. The Somme campaign was to continue for a further four and half months after which the Germans voluntarily withdrew to their newly prepared Hindenberg line early in 1917 and conceded the whole of the bitterly contested Somme front. After a thorough review of the strategy, tactics and commanders, Mr. Middlebrook concludes, *"The only good to emerge from that terrible day was the display of patriotism, courage and self-sacrifice shown by the British soldiers"*. [The First Day on the Somme, Martin Middlebrook, page 292, The Penguin Press, 1971]

Following bitter fighting north of the Somme in 1917, the German Army attacked in a westerly direction in March 1918 passing partly through the blood-soaked Somme battleground pushing the British divisions west towards Amiens. It seemed as though this

A part of the 24 and 25/N.F. of the 34th Division made an incredible advance of 3,000 meters and passed between the now Peake Woods Cemetery and Bailiff Wood in the centre of the picture.

small corner of Picardy would be forever denied to the Allies.

After the Armistice the refugees made their way back to their villages to find but heaps of rubble with hardly a building intact. Blackened stumps were all that remained of the woods in which they used to walk. A lunar landscape of craters, destroyed guns and equipment, dead horses, temporary cemeteries, all the detritus of war must have filled them with horror. They surveyed a scene of total destruction where before, generations had lived happily together. Some were so discouraged they chose to live elsewhere, many settling in the town of Albert where the prospect of finding shelter and work was more promising. Others set about the task of clearing the rubble which was once their home to find some shelter, and the slow process of reconstruction began. Many churches were rebuilt from the original plans retrieved from archives in Amiens and elsewhere.

Nearly sixty years after the Battle of the Somme the 1975 French Census reveals the following housing statistics. It is interesting to compare these with housing figures from 1916 [from the Official History, page 247]:

	Houses in 1916	Houses in 1975 census
Thiepval	93	35
Fricourt	176	166
Montauban-de-Picardie	274	76
Mametz	120	59
Beaumont Hamel	162	89
Longueval	138	97
Contalmaison	72	34
Albert	1105	3975

It can be seen that most of the villages were not fully restored to their pre-war status. Thiepval was a thriving village with a restaurant, café, a few large farms and the imposing château owned by the de Bredas family. On Sundays many people would walk from neighbouring villages to enjoy the view from the Thiepval plateau. From Albert, horse-drawn buses conveyed passengers to the pleasant surroundings of the village.

Of the small villages, only Fricourt resembled its pre-war population. On the other hand the reconstruction of Albert developed continuously and, after a number of years, surpassed its pre-war housing and population.

Today, the Somme is quiet and peaceful and the battlefield has long since returned to agricultural use. It still bears many scars of the conflict. Over eighty years have passed since the battle but each year the plough brings to the surface hundreds of tons of unexploded shells, grenades of all types, shell fragments, shrapnel balls, shell cases, arms and equipment. Sometimes an Allied or German skeleton is found. Since the inauguration in 1932 of the Memorial to the Missing at Thiepval on which over 73,000 names of missing soldiers are etched in stone, the remains of about 300 bodies have been recovered from the battlefield. It is only when one looks at the endless columns of the many faces of the Thiepval Memorial that one even begins to understand the meaning of the word "missing". One asks - how can 73,000 soldiers simply disappear without trace? People come to visit the beautifully kept cemeteries and reflect over the momentous events which took place on this lovely countryside.

On a calm autumn evening, just before dusk, my wife and myself revisited the British military cemetery at Authuille. It is a place we often visit, the cemetery being on a steep curving slope running down to the river Ancre. It is difficult not to be moved to profound thoughts by the headstones, serenity and beauty of this place and, here, Sylvia penned the following lines:

FROM WHENCE THEY CAME

From whence they came, these men of steel.
For the most part boys, turned quickly into men.
Mothers, wives, sisters and sweethearts wept
Finding solace in each others arms,
Not knowing if God had their men kept or slain
To return from whence they came.

Fathers proud of sons, yet inwardly afraid
Of losing them to a foreign land.
At what cost, those who returned?
Broken bodies, tormented minds,
Memories of old pals gone forever,
From whence they came.

And what now, after all these years?
To Flanders fields come kith and kin
To retrace the steps of fallen youth
And pay homage to those men of steel,
And then, fulfilled, return
From whence they came.

Sylvia Cuttell
Authuille, March 1997

ACKNOWLEDGEMENTS

This book is dedicated to Ann and Fred Warren whose gentle but constant persuasion brought about the writing of this guide. My grateful thanks go to Sue Cox for her enthusiastic support, suggestions and help. To Mike Hodgson of Middlebrook-Hodgson Battlefield Tours, whose interest and suggestions have been most helpful. I also wish particularly to thank Dr. G. M. Bayliss, the Keeper of the Department of Printed Books at the Imperial War Museum for authorisation to present the order of battle in a statistical form to suit the format of this guide and for permission to extract other relevant information from the Official History. Reprints of the fourteen volumes of the Official History are available from the Imperial War Museum, Ray Westlake Military Books as well as other sources.

I am indebted to Jim Fallon, PRO of the Gallipoli Association and to his wife Clarice. Jim undertook a thorough reading of the manuscript and his suggestions and comments were very much appreciated. Paul Hanson, the former cartographer of the Western Front Association, Ray Westlake. Paul Reed and Sue Cox who have supplied trench maps and many other friends who have kindly provided information on the location of trenches. Leslie Syree who has the gift of locating original trenches and other sites and who is always more than willing to share his latest find. Billy Ervine of the Somme Association Ltd for supplying me with information and movements of the 36th (Ulster) Division.

During my research over a number of years I have made many friends and contacts. To all, I tend my sincere thanks and although they are too numerous to list, the following have been particularly helpful. Jean-Philippe Leech at the Ulster Tower who always finds time to have a chat and discuss my queries. His father Arthur Leech recently retired from the CWGC after many years service and who has provided information on the CWGC and events in the Thiepval area. Gérard Desailly, the proprietor of the Bellevue camp site in Authuille who, like so many Frenchmen, always finds time to talk about the events on the Somme. His old volume on the First World War provided some interesting material. Bernard Sénéchal, Mayor of Contalmaison and Maurice Miette, Mayor of Fricourt for their help and information obtained from their village archives. Bernard Maes, a Fricourt farmer for taking me to the German concrete protection of the fresh-water well at Fricourt Farm and explaining the relocation of the original Fricourt Farm. Monsieur Lardeur, a Courcelette farmer who always welcomes us and tells us tales handed down to him by his predecessors. After a long tramp over the battlefield it is always pleasant to call in for a refreshing drink at Avril Williams at Auchonvillers or at the visitor's centre at the Ulster Tower where Jean-Philippe not only sells drinks and light refreshment, but also sells books in English. The books are mainly concerned with the 36th (Ulster) Division. Further to the east is the visitor's centre at Delville Wood which Janet and Tom Fairgrieve have been running for a long time and where refreshments are available. They, also, have a good selection of books. Janet always seems to be able to trace a book, postcard or trench I need. To Glynne Payze, a computer buff and friend of many years for his patience and help with disk management. I would like to thank my brother

Raymond who, living in England, was on the spot to find me new addresses, telephone and fax numbers and who was also the first to read the draft of the guide and offer a few suggestions. To my wife Sylvia who, for a very long time now, has had to put up with the table being cluttered with trench maps, IGN maps, books, compass, etc., and, in spite of all this, found the interest and time to help with the drawing of the maps and the proof-reading and also wrote the closing poem in the conclusion.

Finally, I would like to acknowledge two charming elderly French ladies whom my wife and I met last year in Newfoundland Park and who were always surprised and pleased to see so many British and others from far nations come to visit the Somme in such large numbers, even after the passing of so many years. The fact they invited us, complete strangers, to call in at their home in Auchonvillers at any time for a drink and chat, made it quite a moving experience.

Attignat, France March 1997

BIBLIOGRAPHY

(R = reprinted) AND SUGGESTED READING LIST

Official History, Military Operations France & Belgium, 1916, vol. 1	Brigadier-General Sir James E. Edmunds	I.W.M. in assoc. withBattery Press, Nashville 1993 R
First Day on the Somme	Martin Middlebrook	Allen Lane, Penguin Press 1971
The British Campaign in France & Flanders - 1916	Arthur Conan Doyle	Hodder & Stoughton 1918
La Bataille de la Somme	André Laurent	Martelle, Amiens 1996
Somme	Lyn Macdonald	Papermac 1990 R
Somme, Then and Now	John Giles	Battle of Britain Prints International Ltd 1991 R
Before Endeavours Fade	Rose E. B. Coombs	Battle of Britain Prints International Ltd 1994 R
British Battalions on the Somme	Ray Westlake	Leo Cooper, Pen & Sword Books Ltd 1994
Fields of Death	P. Slowe & R. Woods	Robert Hale, London 1990
The Terrors (16th R.I.R.)	Stuart N. White	Somme Association 1996
History of World War I	B. Liddle Hart	Book Club Associates 1979 R
Thiepval	Michael Stedman	Leo Cooper 1995 Pen & Sword Books Ltd
Beaumont Hamel	Nigel Cave	Leo Cooper 1994 Pen & Sword Books Ltd
Serre	J. Horsfall & N. Cave	Leo Cooper 1996 Pen & Sword Books Ltd
The Unending Vigil	Philip Longworth	Leo Cooper in assoc. 1985 R with Secker & Warburg
Battlefield Guide to the Somme	Maj. & Mrs. Holt	Leo Cooper 1996 Pen & Sword Books Ltd
Eye Deep in Hell	John Ellis	Purnell Book Services Ltd 1976

Panorama of the Western Front	John Laffin	Sutton Publishing Ltd 1993
War Walks from Agincourt to Normandy	Richard Holmes	BBC Worldwide Publishing 1996
Verdun/Argonne	Ministère des Beaux Arts	Michelin 1928
Verdun	Jules Romains	Flammarion 1938
When the Barrage Lifts	Gerald Gliddon	Alan Sutton Publishing Ltd 1994 R
Somme Battlefields	M & M Middlebrook	Penguin Books 1994
W.W.1 1914-1918 - The	Peter Simkins	Tiger Books 1994 Western Front International
On the Western Front	John Laffin	Alan Sutton Publishing 1989
Men, Mud and Memorials	Sue Cox	Coquelicots Press 1992 R
Up the line to death, the War poets 1914-1918	Selection by Brian Gardner	Methuen 1995 R

About the Author

Born in 1931 at Alfreton in Derbyshire and educated at Derby College and later at Matlock College of Higher Education, he worked as an office manager for many years in industry before teaching French Language and literature in adult education centres. In 1980 he became a full-time teacher of French and business studies at a comprehensive school in Nottinghamshire.

From his first visit to France in 1958 he became an inveterate francophile and returned each year until his retirement in 1991 when he emigrated to France where he now lives happily with his wife Sylvia in Attignat, a small village some forty miles north of Lyon. He spends a lot of time each year in the Somme furthering his research.

His interests include military history, classical music and French classical literature and a keen interest in computers. For over twenty years he had been researching the twenty six marshals created by Napoléon I under the first French Empire and computerised the thousands of sheets of notes and data of over five hundred Napoleonic battles. In the mid-seventies, after reading Martin Middlebrook's book, *"The First Day on the Somme"* began his interest in the battle of the Somme. This excellent book encouraged the author to further research and, particularly, to trace the steps of his grandfather who served throughout the First World War and was present on the Somme from the very first day.

Many years have passed since then and the author has gradually compiled data on the many aspects of the battle and whereas this guide is relative to the Ist July 1916 only, he hopes to prepare a second guide of a similar format to cover the campaign from the 2nd July to mid-November when very wet conditions brought the campaign to an end.

As reviewed in *The New Chequers,* the journal of the 'Friends of Lochnagar'

148 Days on the Somme
2 July to 26 November 1916
by Barry Cuttell
published by GMS Enterprises
ISBN 1 870384 79 2

With the plethora of battlefield guides that seem to come on the market over the past few years, it takes a rather special effort to capture my interest these days, but Barry Cuttell has succeeded with both his books. Following on from his immensely useful *'One Day on the Somme',* Barry takes up the story of the events on the Somme from 2nd July to the end of November 1916.

This is a book that is scholarly, absolutely invaluable to the battlefield visitor and researcher alike, but it is above all well-written and a fascinating read. The format echoes that of Barry's first guide – a number of statistical listings of divisions, brigades and battalions followed by a description of the infantry attacks. One of the aims of the book is to allow the reader to find the information he wants as quickly and efficiently as possible, and it succeeds admirably.

The author lists more than 1900 trenches and sites incorporating the main infantry objectives; there are concise and clear plans of the objectives; he produces an easy-to-use guide to the panels on the Thiepval Memorial (which as we all know can be most confusing to the uninitiated visitor!); the book contains a wealth of photographs, many of which have rarely been seen before, such as the postcard of Bazentin-le-Grand and the moment of the detonation of Morval church to mention but two. In addition Barry managed to do what few visitors to the Somme can, he gained admittance to High Wood.

"The wood follows the same contours of eighty-three years ago. The battered stumps have disapeared and today fine trees stand close and proud in High Wood. It still has the same impenetrable black sombre appearance viewed either from a distance or close to... if you come to see this place of death, peer into the dark interior, pause and reflect a moment, what you see is the last resting place for more than 8,000 British and German dead."

This is a book to recommend as a vital companion on one's visits to the battlefields, successful because of Barry's depth of knowledge, his love and familiarity with France and the French and his admiration and respect for all who, *"...(stood) witness to the emotive and tumultuous events of the Battle of the Somme?"*

Robert Pike"

available from:
GMS Enterprises
67 Pyhill, Bretton, Peterborough PE3 8QQ
ENGLAND
TEL 01733 265123
email:
GMSAVIATIONBOOKS@COMPUSERVE.COM